Woman—Aware and Choosing

Woman—
Aware and Choosing
Betty J. Coble

Broadman Press/Nashville, Tennessee

For information on how you can become involved in the *Woman—Aware and Choosing* program, either as participant or certified teacher,
write to Ministry of Marriage, P. O. Box 2188,
Westminster, California 92683.

Dewey Decimal Classification: 301.427
Subject Heading: Marriage
Library of Congress Card Number: 75-7943
Printed in the United States of America

To
Harold, my loving husband, who
has helped me find a satisfactory
definition of wife in our relationship

Contents

Foreword

When it comes to a book on human relationships, I like one that is simple and practical. This is just such a book.

I even like the title. In my experience, I find that men, especially after they are married, tend to look on themselves as authorities, and seldom take the time or effort to read a book of this type. So it's up to the woman—and perhaps that is as it should be.

Mrs. Coble gives some simple, down-to-earth, extremely practical advice which, if followed, would help to bring happiness and real harmony into your marriage.

RUTH (MRS. BILLY) GRAHAM
Montreat, North Carolina

Introduction

". . . Requests the honor of your presence at the marriage of our daughter . . ." are some of the most beautiful words in print. I remember (as most women do) all of those special dreams that raced through my mind. Those dreams promised a lifetime of happiness in store because I had found the one and only young man for me.

The bride-to-be envisions all of her needs being met by this young *super* man. She did not choose to be born a female, but when she married she chose to be a wife. Somewhere in reading books, seeing movies, and in girlhood daydreams, she had imagined that one day she would fall in love with a handsome prince charming and he would whisk her off to his lovely apartment or house or castle (depending on how big a dreamer she was).

With the beautiful wedding ceremony she heard him pledging to bring her true happiness forever and ever. The fairy dust magic of love was to make their marriage perfect.

When questioned about where they would live, there was always a quick response that anywhere would be great as long as they were together. When some doubting one inquired about job and finances she mused that two can live better than one because they can share the expenses. Sharing would never be a problem for them because they love each other and they are marrying on a 50-50 basis. Mother's point that there were differences in background or faith that need to be worked out before marriage were pushed aside. There was the reply, "We have talked about all those kinds of things and there are no problems." In her mind the bride-to-be was very sure that all of these areas would never be a point of contention because of the *fact of marriage.*

11

Rude awakening! Wedding over. Ink dried on marriage license and some kind of poison sets in—instead of "anywhere he wants to live is OK as long as we are together," there is a questioning as to "why do we have to make this move? I like it here. This is where you said we would live after we were married."

Instead of sharing in the financial obligations, there is the struggle for control or the constant reminder that there is never enough money for anything. Instead of differences being settled she comments, "I assumed you would . . . I didn't know you were . . . I thought you loved me . . ." Where is that *and they lived happily ever after* she has dreamed about all of her young life? All she ever wanted was a happy marriage and she cannot understand why it is not *happening* to her.

Her words are changed from Aisle, Altar, and Hymn to *I'll Alter Him.*

Deep down a woman comes to marriage with plans all her own to remodel what she does not like in her young man—without giving it a thought that he may object. She has bright hopes of changing all of *his* habits, *his* ideas, *his* mannerisms and other things that are in conflict with *her* own.

The choice to become a wife is made with vague knowledge of what is involved in the commitment. There was a time when parents made the commitment for the young people who had practically no choice on their part. There was also a time when a wife was sold to the highest bidder or given by a father as a favor to someone he wished to impress. These plans were secretive and forced upon the woman regardless of her own personal desire.

This is not the case today. While the bride-to-be does not have to work out a relationship that is not of her own choosing, she is asked to work out a relationship with little, if any, information about what it takes to *build* a happy marriage.

The bride enters marriage with scant knowledge, one-time counseling, and very poor patterns to follow. To put it mildly, she enters a state of confusion and seeks to find her own way through the maze. She is hoping all the way that she will somehow find fulfillment in marriage by just "staying with it."

There is not a single endeavor a woman enters into in which she has as little *real* information as she does for marriage. If she were choosing a career she would find out the qualifications and the remunerations. She enters marriage as if it takes no information or qualifications. This is one reason for such a high failure rate.

The worth and identity of a wife are being questioned on every hand. There is not a female this is not affecting. Today, many wives are in the working force. They are trying to find meaning and fulfillment for themselves. One of the reasons for the term *"just a housewife"* is that many women have sought to say who they are by how others see them and how they feel about their own value as persons. Today's value system dictates "no monetary value—no worth."

Women do not want to feel worthless. Whether she is working outside the home or inside the home, or both, the key is cooperating with, not competing with, her husband. Struggling to do anything, especially a career, when there is dissension between husband and wife is too taxing. She must convey to her husband that she wants to work outside the home to fulfill a need, not because there is a lack in him. When we allow freedom, we gain freedom.

For survival she paints her own picture and begins the remodeling job mentally. Her list of things that would make her happy if *he* would do them for *her* goes something like this: *if he* would change *his* habits . . . *if he* would buy a new . . . *if he* would treat *her* the way *she* wants to be treated . . . *if he* would . . . *if he* would . . . *if he would only* . . . if he would treat her the way she wants to be treated . . . if he would just try to understand why she wants to work . . .

Oh where, oh where has her happiness gone? "Right out of the window" *if she* was depending on her husband for her happiness, for he does not have happiness to give her.

Sensible solutions are available—contrary to what many today would try to make us believe. I am much aware that some seriously feel that marriage is a hopeless endeavor. There is a constant output of negativism about marriage by many wives who—at the same time—are keeping up a front by saying their marriage is "fine."

What they are really saying is that they have as good a marriage as anyone else they know. For a sampling of this, think back on the last bridal shower you attended. Try to remember how much, if any, encouragement the bride was given. All of the put down of marriage was in a joking manner, but nevertheless the discontent was evident. A great number of deeply hurting wives are listening to and searching for answers from the many voices which claim they have the key.

In 1940 Dale Carnegie said that if we had more education on sex we would have better marriages (at that time 16 out of 100 were ending in divorce). Book upon book has tried to spell out definitely that this is why a woman's marriage is not satisfying. Thirty-five years later, with sex volume upon sex volume available and supposedly read, we are on a ratio of 50 out of 100 dissolutions of marriage. In Orange County, California, in 1974 for the first time ever there were more dissolutions of marriage applied for than licenses for marriage.

Other observers have said that the needed adjustment is to be able to communicate better. Many a wife has studied the art of listening and has come to better understand and appreciate the man she has married. She has found that marriages are not built on talking and listening alone.

One of the loud voices demanding attention is saying, "The thing a wife needs is to have an equal place with her husband." When she can have "equal pay with equal say," she will be happy. This voice says if she competes with man she will come out the winner, because she is willing to compete.

Other voices claim no woman can be happy and stay at home doing "menial tasks" all day long. What a wife needs is a career of her own, and she needs to assert herself. They say happiness is in freedom to do as she pleases.

It is suggested by some that the problem may be the idea of *one man, one woman, for life.* They tell her that it would be helpful to have a re-designing of the overall pattern of marriage. This recommendation is *Open Marriage* with no binding agreements. Each part is free, as though single, to cultivate friendships that may or may not include sexual relationships.

Some prompt her to consider the need for *Series* marriage so life would not be so boring. This advice is for the purpose of checking to see if she would like to be married and there are to be *no* children. The second state, and possible second contract with a different partner, is for the purpose of rearing children. This stage is to last until the children are adults. Act three of the series would give another option to change partners "as they waltz through the carefree middle years." The final act is the time to choose the man with whom she would like to spend her retiring years.

One style that has been popular for years is that of *changing partners*. This one says: what is wrong is she made a poor choice in the first place. The husband is just not doing his part. If you will notice in most of these situations, *his part* is defined by *her*.

The woman who has a happy marriage seems fearful to speak up because the loud cries of the desperately unhappy woman make her question if there is more that she is not aware exists.

Take courage, wife, whether in the camp of the timid, happy, or the vocal unhappy. Finding happiness is "one more" difficult search. The most valuable relationship on this earth is that of husband and wife. Only when marriage is viewed as a valuable possession will one give it the attention and care that is needed. Only then will it grow into a relationship that will be satisfying to both partners. I have a beautiful ring that my husband gave me for my birthday, and I find it completely loses its brilliance unless I spend some time caring for it. A good marriage takes effort.

There are three sources of help I would offer a wife for maintaining her marriage or discovering what makes a happy marriage—her husband, the Scriptures, and my own experience.

Her Husband, though untrained and unskilled in building a relationship with a wife, is trying to tell her what his needs are in relationship to her. Referring back to what she has seen and what she has heard from other women—whether in words or attitudes—it is very difficult to listen to what *he* is saying to *her*. After all, he is "only a man" and what does he know about marriage?

He probably has not even read a recent book or article on under
standing *her*.

Remember it is *his* marriage, *too*, and he just may want very
much to build a special, close relationship with the woman he
has chosen. The clues she needs are being stated or have been
stated over and over again. A listening ear turned to him would
be quite revealing.

Wife, do you want a standard to live by, regardless of what
others are doing around you? When the majority is saying there
are no answers because there are so many divorces among those
we thought had good marriages. The age-old instructions by the
manufacturer himself are passed over, because they have been
misinterpreted or misused, and very few have ever seen them put
into practice. They are nonetheless valid today.

. . . Satan speaking, "Did God say . . .?" And the wheels began
to turn and Eve began to wonder if God really had her best interest
at heart. All of the offers sounded *sooo* attractive and looked *sooo*
beautiful. The best part of all was: if she took advantage of the
opportunity before her—she would be *equal—equal* with God, no
less.

The choice did not seem so difficult. "The more you know, the
better off you are," is good reasoning. But the devil did not tell
all, as usual. Knowledge without understanding breeds rebellion.
This defiance of God's authority brought restrictions upon woman-
kind. We call that "the curse."

In this book I wish to offer you some ideas that I have found
helpful in my own 29-year marriage, ideas that have been shared
in a weekday class with over a thousand women over the past
five years. If I seem one sided be assured you are reading me
as I intended. This is written to a woman who has chosen to be
a wife or intends to become a wife, or is divorced and would like
to pick up her own worth as an individual. Because I have written
it for *you*, I see no need to include the husband's responsibilities
since he is not likely to be reading this book. And if you told
him *again* he still would not listen to your instruction. Let's stay
in our own area where we can actually do many determining things.

A wife who tries to understand the responsibilities of a husband, in order to direct him, will totally miss the happiness and fulfillment of being a wife.

Here is a list of things you will need while reading this book:

Your own book	so you can mark in it for further reference. The concepts need to be re-thought.
Several weeks	not because you are a slow reader but because you need time to think and argue with me mentally.
Paper and pencil	I would suggest that you hide the pencil so you do not have to spend half of your reading time searching for it and write in your book if paper is scarce at your house.
An open mind	so you can think through the ideas presented here and see if you have a need in a particular area. Every area needs examination but every area does not necessarily need change.
A willingness to try something different for a change	I am not suggesting a *new* husband but a new way of looking at the *old* one.

Basic Needs of a Wife
in Marriage

1
Basic Needs of a Wife in Marriage

"What happened to my marriage? I have given him the best years of my life and now he says we have no reason to stay together. There must be some things that I have done right! Why isn't he ever satisfied?" Sound familiar?

One woman meets one man and they desire to commit themselves to marriage and become *bonded* together *by God* and *much effort* on their part *to become one.*

I don't want to oversimplify a very complex problem, but I feel there are areas which we fail to consider when we talk about building a happy marriage.

I want to discuss five basic needs a woman has in marriage if she is to fill the *wife* part to her satisfaction.

1. She needs to identify *who she is and like herself.*
2. She needs to decide what she wants out of her marriage.
3. She needs to learn to communicate with her husband.
4. She needs to feel the love of her husband.
5. She needs to find fulfillment in her marriage.

The desire to be free, to be all we want to become is in each of us. Identity is an extremely real need.

Robbed of Identity? New efforts are being made to keep one's maiden name after all the years of waiting to be Mrs. "whatever his name is." Why?

Many a young bride lays down her identity of single woman at the altar of marriage, expecting the new husband to pick it up and tell her who she is *now*. Months and even years go by. One day she awakens with an identity crisis on her hands. "I don't know who I am" or "I'm a nothing in this family."

She has not been robbed of her identity; she stopped being

21

responsible for *herself* and, without even discussing it with her husband, she started expecting him to *work out her life for her.*

"All I want is to be independent, secure, and happy" is the way Joan, an emotional 30-year-old wife, stated it.

Everyone wants to feel that she is an important part of whatever she chooses to do. When a woman has chosen to be a wife, she has chosen what position she will operate from in furthering her own search for identity.

She is responsible for working out her own definition of what is involved in being a good wife in her own marriage situation. She cannot live by an outside definition.

When two people play the game of tennis they are of equal importance to the game. The rules say one person on each side of the net. The purpose of the game is to serve and return the ball until the game is won. Can you imagine player "A" (wife) serving the ball to player "B" (husband) and then running to player "B's" side of the court and telling him how to return the ball? How could player "A" ever return to her side of the court in time to return the ball for which she is responsible?

Part of the frustration a woman feels in marriage is at the point of trying to decide who she is by running all over the court playing both sides of the marriage.

"Who am I?" must be answered to her satisfaction before she will ever be able to define the position of wife.

Her Side of the Court. A wife is responsible *only* for being the wife and in no way is she responsible for being the husband. She is rejecting the idea on every hand that she is to be the one that holds the marriage together. It takes *two* to commit marriage and there are two distinct areas of responsibility that must be decided on by the *wife and the husband together.*

Is it possible for a couple to go from California to New York *together* if the wife takes a southern route and the husband takes a northern route? No way! Yet many are trying to have a happy marriage, not recognizing the need for two distinct individuals to plan together which way they want to travel through life.

A wife should take the time to discover the positive side of her own personality. She is worth knowing for the fact of *who she is,* and who she is is exactly what she has to bring to marriage.

We do not like for our friends to criticize us and find fault with the way we see things and the way we do things. The least a wife should do is be a friend to herself and stop tearing herself down and spend her energies discovering *who she is now* as a wife.

How much a wife *likes herself* determines what kind of eyes she is seeing her husband through. If critical of herself, then she will be passing judgment constantly on her husband. If she is unsure of herself she will not allow her husband the privilege of having different ideas or opinions than those of her own. These negative thought patterns about her own worth become actions that gnaw on her marriage relationship. A woman unhappy with herself is limiting herself to having an unhappy marriage.

What's in it for me? Until a wife decides what she wants to gain from her marriage she will not know whether or not she is successful. She cannot draw up a plan of action until she knows what she wants. To have the desire for a happy marriage without looking at what makes her happy is a sure road to disappointment.

Dr. Theodore Isaac Rubin in a recent article in the *Journal* said that happiness is what the majority of people are looking for when they seek counseling.

Women are trying to buy happiness in involvement, in things like clothes, houses, careers, and children. Happiness is not available from without but must come from within. It is up to the wife to *make her own happiness.*

Many a husband has come to the point of desperation trying to make his wife happy—only to find that anything he did for her was not enough unless she decided to be happy in receiving his gestures of kindness.

What does she need as a wife? The list of needs that she makes for herself is important. Listing needs usually ends up with a "I need a new coat" kind of inventory. "Things" are secondary needs. What a wife needs is to be able to share *who she is* and *what she thinks* and *how she feels.* This is a skill that must be learned.

Let's talk. Okay. We talk about the children. We talk about the house or car. We talk about the neighborhood or the nation or the world. What a wife is in real need of is to talk *about herself.* How does a husband know what his wife's needs are unless *she* tells him?

Doing what comes "natural" she begins, "I think *you should*" or "I feel *you should*" or "I want *you to*"—and as far as her husband is concerned he is totally deaf. He is not in the least interested in her telling *him* what *he should* be doing. He is keenly interested in what *she thinks,* what *she feels, who she is,* and what *she needs.*

Feeling loved is one need that causes a woman to desire marriage. She wants to be the one and only love of her husband's life. She desires to *feel* warmth toward him and a closeness that spells belonging. She takes quite seriously the "leaving all others for her alone" in the wedding ceremony.

Most husbands have said by proposing marriage that they love her above all others and want to build a life with her alone. There are a number of ways that a husband expresses his love. Between sobs Becky asked, "After 25 years of marriage if he really loved me, wouldn't he have to say it sometime?"

A wife needs to realize what her husband is saying to her when he has commited himself to providing food, clothing, home, health care, recreation . . . When he comes home day in and day out he is saying, "It is you I love." Does she comment to him each time he comes home how much she appreciates the fact that he has returned home to her? Many times she is criticizing *him* for not verbalizing about her contribution and how important she is to him, instead of doing something about herself.

A wife must learn to accept her husband's love as he chooses to express it to her. Pat's husband in desperation, trying to escape her constant reminders that he was not expressive enough to please her, asked if she would be willing to exchange temperament traits for a two-week period. She agreed. He was to be as she had requested: kissing her, always touching her, and verbalizing his "I love you's" often. In return she was not to initiate any of the expressions that were so important to her. By the end of one week she was begging him to change back . . . because she could not stand *not expressing herself as she really was.* He insisted that they carry out the two-week commitment to impress upon them both the need for freedom to be themselves in expressing love.

In a complaining voice Martha said, "My husband isn't romantic anymore. He never brings me flowers or candy or any other gifts except on birthdays and anniversaries and Christmas and . . . Well, he acts like it is a real treat if we go out for a hamburger." Romance to him is having her totally with him. *Presence.* This is difficult for a wife when romance to her has been in things. *Presents.* The places he has taken her and the things he has done for her are of primary importance to her. He is continuing to do for her but in a different way.

"If he loves me so much why can't I feel his love?" Joyce quibbled. Where does his love get lost? When a husband is giving and the wife is not receiving, both are lonely. When a friend wishes to give a gift on a birthday we do not dictate to her what it will be. Nor do we refuse to receive it, if it is not to our liking, unless we want to lose a friend quickly. There are only two alternatives when we are presented a gift. We either *accept* it as given or we are *rejecting* it.

A husband's love must be accepted as he chooses to give it, or we are refusing it by stating the terms of the gift.

Benjamin Franklin said, "If you would be loved, love and be lovable." Giving love seems to be a prerequisite to having assurance that you are loved. We need a very clear definition of love so we will know what we are supposed to be giving away and receiving.

Fulfillment: today's word. Fulfillment is a word in the conversation of most wives today. A wife must know her own needs and have some goals for her marriage to share with her husband before she can find fulfillment. She comes as a *contributing part* this way and not to have everything done *for* her.

Every woman has a need to feel that what she is spending her life on is important. Because there is no dollar value placed on what a wife contributes and no yearly efficiency report, she is referred to as *"just a housewife."* This has an adverse affect on the woman who already feels cheated in her position or who does not like herself.

The wife who sees her worth in relationship to her husband sees the house as only a small part of her responsibility. She realizes she is not imprisoned by four walls and married to the house *unless she chooses to be.* She has as much freedom to define her role as a wife as she desires along with the husband she has chosen. As she spells out her own role she gains a sense of self worth and a sense of accomplishment.

To be needed by her husband does not necessarily mean she is fulfilled. Being needed to the extent that others dictate the use of all her time is not a healthy situation. Too much demand on her time leads to resentment. She can be *needed* to death.

A wife who sees herself as a spare tire, only to meet the needs of her husband, soon gets the door-mat complex. "Poor-me-all-I-ever-do-is" . . . syndrome. In her own estimation she is filling the slot of a servant and becoming angrier with herself all of the time she is allowing this to be her way of life. This anger becomes resentment. The effort to keep her resentment hidden bursts forth in tension and frustration.

Fulfillment is accomplished by being in charge of her own time. Choosing what to do, scheduling a time to do it, and doing the task are her responsibilities.

Frustration comes to the wife who lets the demands of those around her dictate her priorities and work time. The neighborhood gals over the back fence or over a cup of coffee, the friend that prefers to talk about how irresponsible her husband is (instead of doing her own work), the committee member over the phone that just must get to the tasks of her day—all coax her away from being in charge of her own time.

A big part of feeling worthwhile is how a wife looks at the routine, mundane necessities that must be done. She can dread them or put them off until she has used up all of her energy *or* she can learn to complete them knowing how good she feels about the remainder of her day.

"To be bored or not to be bored" is each wife's decision. It is not forced on anyone. She can feel accomplishment if she chooses.

A giant step is made toward finding worth as a wife when she assumes responsibility for her own happiness. Happiness is not something that can be given to her as a gift. Rather it is a precious commodity that she must search for and find for herself. It is only available to her as she learns to look for it in her own circumstances and with the assurance that she is deserving of happiness.

Fulfillment is not found in filling all of the hours in a day with things that are meaningless to her or that drive away her loneliness.

For two hours one evening I sat in an informal group for young wives and shared some areas of adjustment I felt would be helpful in marriage. I made the statement that when you become a wife you do not become responsible for how your husband acts. He is responsible for what he says, his own manners, what he chooses to do, and how he spends his time. He is an adult, also. He did not marry to have judgment passed on him or for correction.

When I had finished that evening Jane, a bride of six months, said, "Until this evening I had decided that I could not go on with my marriage because my husband just refused to change, and he is too much responsibility for me."

Where is the most miserable place in the world? It is the place where we say by our condemnation that we are right and anyone who differs with us just has to be wrong. The weight is much too heavy to bear when we try to transfer our standards into another person's life—when the other person has no desire to change.

Identifying herself and liking who she is, knowing her own needs and being able to communicate them to her husband, feeling loved, and finding fulfillment in marriage are all possible for the woman of *today* . . . even in the midst of all the clamoring about marriage being an impossible dream.

William Lederer in *The Mirages of Marriage* says, "Just as much work, energy, strength and time is required to support a bad marriage as to support a good one."

Regardless of how equal a wife may become, or how much success and acclaim she may have, there is nothing that will bring her more lasting fulfillment than spending her time, energy, and talent building a good relationship with her husband.

Identity Crisis

2
Identity Crisis

Whether you address her mail *Ms.* or *Mrs.* is *not* the issue. What each woman thinks and feels about herself *is* important.

"Who am I?" is often answered with, "I really don't know anymore. I have lost my identity. I feel like a maid in this house. How can you feel worthwhile or important in your life when all you do is pick up your husband's socks or close the drawers he leaves open?" This attitude is a serious thing in any marriage.

What has caused woman to begin the fight for her rights on such a low level? It could be that she is fed up with trying to live out her life by someone else's vague definition. *Or* she has not given consideration to where she wants to go in her marriage. *Or* she is trying to gain happiness in marriage from the husband side of the marriage. The real problem more likely is she *does not like herself.*

Dr. Maxwell Maltz in *The Magic Power of Self Image Psychology* says that 95 per cent of us suffer from an inferiority complex. We spend the majority of our time putting ourselves down. We criticize ourselves about everything we do, and we seldom feel we have really done as well as we should have done in any given situation. We are calling on *self* for a perfect performance in order to feel we are acceptable.

I did my own mini-survey of 250 women over the past year and asked each one, "What is your number one need as a person?" They have responded in unison that they do not like who they are today. As Chris, an attractive woman in her thirties, put it, "I do not like the way I am; I do not like the things that are happening to me. I feel like a complete failure. I am really a nothing."

31

Labels she operates under. When she allows others to identify her, she ends up with "she is so and so's daughter—Mr. so and so's wife—Tom's or Susie's mother." That is great but that only tells me *where* she operates, not *who she is.* Labels are fine for identifying the package, but content is pivotal, especially in "getting her head on straight" as far as *who she is.*

Women who are seeking to identify themselves and check their own worth are the brunt of many jokes. Yet if a woman continues to perform as a *good* daughter, wife, mother, teacher, social worker, or whatever *to satisfy others* she will end up a bitter, critical, unhappy little old lady that absolutely *no* one wants to be around.

Labels are great if the person behind them is doing her own defining of her role and making her own choices as she goes.

Stuck with me or privileged to be me. "You are what you have been given to work with" was the subject of the discussion the morning Sue moved toward me in tears. "I really feel that I have been short-changed because you can see what a mess I am." True, I saw a sad, dejected, unhappy wife with what looked like very little going for her. We came to the conclusion after a few minutes that she would have to live with *herself* all of her life, so she must begin to work with what she had been given.

There is no way that we can bypass our *self*-evaluation and work on building a happy marriage. A woman has *only herself to contribute* to a relationship. Most of the time she thinks it would be easier to begin by getting her husband straightened out or working on the circumstances around her. This leads to learning how to manipulate the husband and brings a great deal of satisfaction for a period of time—but does not bring a lasting happiness. "I complimented my husband and he really responded to me and was in a happy mood for several days, *but* he never compliments me, so I just gave up," was Margaret's evaluation of manipulation. It is a dangerous business to try changing a husband instead of working on your own self-esteem.

Working *on* others or *for* others may leave a wife behind while everyone in the household goes their separate ways, working out their happiness in their own worlds and leaving *her* very empty.

What about *her?*

Self-criticism is easy at this point—but deadly. There is little effort required in criticizing *self.* It is a natural and acceptable thing to do. When we practice looking at what we are doing wrong instead of what we are doing right, we are not even aware of how we are treating *self.* In our house we refer to this as "counting the empties."

Jesus told us to get our *total person* involved in loving God, loving *self,* and loving others. We are made for loving. All areas of life need love and to love *others* as we love *self* is to be the standard. This is usually thought of in a very self-sacrificing way, and we try to force *self* to love others.

The value is placed on *self*-love. The standard for giving love is determined by how a person feels about *self.*

Throughout the Scriptures we are admonished to be fair, just, honest, forgiving, considerate, thoughtful, generous, accepting, friendly, and loving to others. Before these can be practiced toward another they must be used toward *self.*

When constantly criticizing *self* it will be awfully difficult to find worthwhile points in others. If we cannot be honest with *self* and face the areas that ought to be changed, we will be taking others apart in order to justify our own need for improvement.

Being considerate with others sometimes seems much easier than being kind to *self.* When we accept our imperfections and quit trying to become perfect "in six easy lessons," then we will be much more relaxed toward others.

What a wife has done for *herself* in the past week tells her something about how worthwhile she sees *herself* as being. She can best see the needs of others if she spends some time on *self.*

Generosity is an attitude that is grown when a person does not cheat *self.* Being stingy and always scrimping on things done for *self,* in order that others may have more, develops a martyr complex. This adds to the storage of resentment which becomes an irritant in a marriage.

Accepting *self and liking* much of what you see does not say you are satisfied to stay the same for your entire life. Rather it is recognizing what is right and good as you are today and working from there.

Encouraging friends and affirming what they have accomplished builds a good relationship. A compliment to *self* will do you no harm.

Risky Business—Identity. We have built-in fears that have been drilled into us from the *misteaching* of what humility is all about. Humility is versus conceit in most of our minds. Elaine's statement, "I never could sing that song. I just am not good enough," is a good example of what some people call humility. The opposite of that is Connie's presumptuous, "I am better than anyone who sings that song." This seems to be the two choices that we offer *self* when we think of *liking self.* To *like self* does *not* mean arrogant conceit which is a mask behind which a person with an inferior feeling hides.

Putting *self* down does *not* mean humility. Rather, it says we think God did not make *all* people, *only some* people, important. Humility is not to be confused with low self-esteem. Humility is *not* putting *self* down or letting others walk over us or treat us in a wrong way.

A humble person is unassuming, without arrogance, submissive, and obedient. To obey or submit suggests that person has willingly given over to someone she feels is worthy of her commitment. We might say she has a right evaluation of *herself* in the light of God's opinion of her. *Liking self* is the way to become an unassuming person. The other alternative is to be fighting and manipulating all the while to have her own way.

A wife cannot be all that she wants to be in the marriage unless she is giving credit to *self* for the contribution she is making to the marriage.

All she has to offer. Why Am I Afraid to Tell You Who I Am? by John Powell gives a very concise answer. "I am afraid to tell you who I am, because, if I tell you who I am, you may not like who I am, and it's all that I have." This fear is one that causes a closing up of the real person in a lonely shell.

A wife's desire to be accepted by her husband is so strong that the fear he will not like her prevents a deep sharing of *self.* This is especially true if a wife is critical and judgmental of her husband rather than being honest about *herself.*

The person she really *is* is worth knowing. She can be honest all day about *self.* This does not mean that she ought to tell every thought she has, but she should express how she *feels* and what she *thinks* and what she *needs* in relationship to her husband.

In order to share *self* with her husband she must know something about his ideas, desires, needs, and how he feels about himself. Just being together does not accomplish this. Two people can live in the same house and do little more than annoy one another!

The sharing of *self* with her husband calls for the risk of being hurt, disappointed, or totally misunderstood. If the venture seems too hazardous she may choose to build barriers for protection instead of lines for further communication.

It is not necessary to wait for your husband to initiate the sharing. You can begin. Your interest and concern should be in what you need to tell him about *yourself.* This kind of an approach is giving all you have to offer and the response of your husband is not your responsibility.

Many women feel like they have tried to share who they are with their husband only to feel rejected. At second glance they find that what they have really shared is how disappointed or angry they are with the way *he* is behaving as a husband.

The sharing of *who she is* should begin from the *positive* side.

Maybe I'm not so special. Another real fear is: if there is no *self*-criticism, there will be no motivation to improve. There is a place for looking at ourselves and acknowledging our need for improvement. The wrong is in repeatedly belittling *self* instead of making plans for the improvement that is essential.

The constant comparison of *self* with another is unfair because God made no duplicates. No duplicate person—so, therefore, no duplicate assignment.

HOW-TO KIT FOR LIKING WHO SHE IS

What does a wife do when she realizes that she does not like much about *herself?* (So that you might remember what you have to work with I would like to compare your "kit for liking *self*" with making a dress.)

Step one—right fabric furnished. Everyone who sews knows that choosing just the right material says what the finished garment will look like, feel like, and fit like.

Who is responsible for this individual, unique, beautiful, and important person in the beginning? The Psalmist states it well when he says that we are fearfully and wonderfully made, or, in other words, wonderfully complex with marvelous workmanship and special design.

God created her and gave her life with the cooperation of her parents. He placed her in the family where he wanted her to grow, so she would be prepared for the special assignment he has given to her. She is unique in that God made *only one* exactly like her. We laughingly comment that the reason there is only one is because the world could not stand two! Not so! It is because there is no place for two people trying to fill exactly the same role. If you can, imagine two women trying to give birth to the same child. Impossible? True. You are a person born to live throughout eternity as a person. This person is an ever-growing, changing, becoming *individual.*

Beautiful? Beauty is determined by what you are looking for in a person. Is the gauge of beauty the skin tone or softness, the color of hair and eyes, the shape of body? The outside only says if a person is good looking or glamorous. I grew up with the cliché that "beauty is only skin deep," but who wants to try to survive without skin? Proverbs says outside beauty is vain. Winning all the beauty contests from Miss America down is no assurance of genuine beauty or happiness.

The best judge of a beautiful person is God. He made beautiful flowers and no one criticizes him for that. We do not have to compare a rose with a chrysanthemum in order to see the beauty of the rose. Just suppose the rose said to God it was not satisfied but wanted to be a chrysanthemum. If God should grant the request of the rose and it became a chrysanthemum, it would immediately lose its identity as a rose.

We are made by God's design. Who is to condemn his handiwork?
Herbert B. Barks, Jr., put in this way:

>Believe it
>You are a real find,
>a joy in someone's heart
>You're a jewel, unique and priceless.
>I don't care how you feel.
>Believe it
>God don't make no junk.

Step two—Pattern with instruction guide. We choose a pattern style
that is complimentary to our particular figure and that fits the
occasion.

The pattern reads: beautiful person, made in God's image, special
place of being a wife, potential for growth, talents included, with
choice of arrangement.

The occasion was laid out along with her creation in the form
of *sealed orders.* Unless she follows the instruction sheet step by
step the garment does not fit together smoothly. She is given
understanding to proceed only after she has completed the present
step. She has been given the necessary overall layout. There is
order to her life when she follows through a step at a time, instead
of wishing the dress were ready to wear just because she has the
fabric and pattern.

"This doesn't seem like a very special place to me. I'm not even
sure I married the right man," was the comment of Mildred in
a group discussion on the privileges of being a wife. To learn to
like *herself* she must begin where she is today and recognize this
is the base she must work from. I do not know a single wife who
has perfect circumstances to work under, but every wife I know
has a place *all her own.*

God brought Eve to Adam and presented her to him. This should
show us a bit of the importance of the place of a wife. The tradition
of a father bringing the bride to the altar is still carried on today.

Some women find the place of wife to be the greatest possible
position for them. The challenge of constructing this association
into something meaningful to both husband and wife is over-

whelming. The privilege of becoming a mother and sharing in the molding of lives is awesome. The free time to develop her own interests and talents is inviting.

And there is more. The Bible presents an organization that is fantastic and is yet to be improved. God in his wisdom has made every part of this universe with perfect order, and he has not left woman out. He instructed man to be the leader; woman to complete, complement, and follow; children to be trained, enjoyed, and sent out from the home.

Logic reasons that any business, in order to survive, must have a leader. Within this structure of leadership a wife has: the provision of love, guidance that is with her own interest in mind, and someone with whom she may completely share herself. A leader and lover all rolled into one!

The instruction sheet says to the wife that she is to become a *willing, participating follower.*

Step three—Necessary equipment. Scissors, pins, tape measure, chalk—small things but absolutely necessary to making a dress.

Not only a place all her own but the abilities, with potential of becoming all that she needs to be to fill her purpose. These several abilities call for work which only she can do. God does not create individuals without potentially equipping them for the job. He intended that marriage be a happy, fulfilling relationship for one's life.

We have a tendency to think of abilities or talents as things someone else can see us performing and applaud. We simply assume if we do not have a performing art we have *no* talent. Have you ever said of another person that he just has a knack for making you feel at ease? Or I enjoy being around so and so because they are so friendly? In my estimation these are two abilities that are high on my list of desirables.

Every person has some quality that they can develop to give them satisfaction and to benefit others around them.

What capabilities does she bring to this position of wife? Is it a good disposition, neatness, organization, thrift, intelligence, education, promptness, creativeness, studious interest, appreciation of others, or what? When we begin with what we have most of the time we are surprised how much God has given us with which to work.

A most helpful Scripture is the one on talents found in the book of Matthew. The person that holds on to her talent for fear of not having enough will go through life in want. But the person who uses or develops the talent that God gave will find there is no end of raw material with which to work.

When I started teaching I would come from a class and feel so undone that I relived every minute with, "I should have said this or I should have reacted another way." I would be awake all hours of the night rehashing every detail. In the midst of one of those "Why aren't you perfect?" sessions I had an idea. It occurred to me that I could not do that session over but I could learn from the experience. Now I practice an evaluation of the class and file in my "mini-computer" what was good and reuseable and discard what was ineffective.

Step four—ready to sew. Fabric, pattern, necessary equipment, and now she is ready to put it all together. Making her own garment.

The day a wife accepts the fact that she is not responsible for her husband's actions is one of the greatest days of her life. If he uses the wrong fork or refuses to respond as *she thinks he should* it is no reflection on her. The wife is not responsible for the husband side of the marriage, *but* she *is* responsible for *all* of the *wife* side of marriage.

When a wife starts trying to operate from the husband side of the marriage she misses the joys of being a wife. This is carried over in relation to the children when mothers insist that fathers feel, think, and act like mothers. Children do not need two mothers. They need mother and father.

There are many intriguing areas in being a wife that simply cannot be explored if she is all hung up on trying to *make* a good husband.

Step five—custom made—choices unlimited—finish when ready. Wishing I had something to wear is not enough. I must complete the necessary work before I can enjoy what I have made.

One of the beautiful facets about being made in the image of God is the choices he leaves to us. We are responsible for what we choose, but we are free to choose. If something we try in building the relationship does not work we are not trapped in failure, but we have the ability to evaluate and choose another method or time.

This is the hardest part of sewing to most of us. We would prefer beginning a new garment rather than having to rip out something that is wrong and doing it over. Taking out what does not fit is absolutely necessary if we are to be happy with wearing the dress. Also, it is mandatory that we remove the hindrances to building a good relationship, even though it is time-consuming and sometimes painful for a while.

Because of the freedom of choice we have the right to change the direction of our own lives. A wife does not have this right over her husband or any other person. God so designed us to be in control of *ourselves*. When a wife has the desire to change or control her husband she should think about how precious her own choice is to her.

(Stop reading here until you have listed at least two things you *like* about *yourself*. Add to the list as you read on until you have at least twenty things you like about yourself. What do I mean? I want you to take a good look at yourself and write down the traits you have that you would compliment a friend for if you saw the same qualities in her. By doing this you will begin to use your *kit for liking self* as well as *identifying self*.)

Most people are looking for an investment that will pay fantastic dividends with no risk. I suggest one to every wife. Begin today to learn to like yourself better. In order to accomplish this you must stay in the right time zone. I have used three important words: *begin, learn, today*.

Yesterday is gone and there is nothing we can do to recall it. Tomorrow is not yet ours because it is not here. *Today* is the only time we have to profit from yesterday's mistakes and plan toward tomorrow.

"I am exhausted from digging, digging, digging all of the way back to my great-grandmother to find out what she did wrong, so I can blame her for the way my marriage is falling apart. Tell me what I can do about it today," was the plea of Delores, a young wife—with several small children—who was falling apart emotionally.

We have some temperament traits that are born in us. However, there is not a temperament trait which does not have its strengths as well as weaknesses. We can cultivate the bad qualities and neglect the good if that is *our* choice. I do not know anyone that has a perfect set of ancestors or perfect circumstances, but I do know many people who are building a good relationship in marriage. And they do not choose to let what their great-grandpa did ruin today.

Be yourself. There are times when all of us feel that if we could only be someone else we could make a good life for ourselves.

Frustration is the result when we are constantly comparing ourselves with another woman to see if we are acceptable. The person we pick for comparison is often the best in the field. There is nothing cheap about comparison. If a woman wants to know if she is well dressed, she usually picks the millionaire's wife with which to compare. If she wants to compare her creative abilities, she checks to see how she measures up with *House Beautiful.*

It is a well-known fact that most women do not choose to dress alike. A woman is furious if she buys a new dress and finds that someone else has chosen the same dress for the same occasion.

A wife should enjoy being *herself* and begin to work with what she has been given. Does that mean that a wife can do whatever she wants to do? *Yes.* Most women would like to lose ten pounds *today*, and buy a new wardrobe, and take a vacation to the place of their choice all at one time. Daydreams! The problem is a woman wants to arrive where she is going before she has made any plans to go.

Take the ten pounds she wants to lose. When she gets on the bathroom scales the morning after she has decided to lose the weight, does she expect it to be gone? Does she feel disappointed that it has not melted away overnight? Or does she start with breakfast and plan what she is *not* going to eat in order to lose part of a pound each day until all ten pounds are gone?

If she is serious she realizes that she *cannot* lose an ounce until she chooses to do so. She decides what weight she will be, what she will wear, and in what attitude she will travel. She chooses whether she will be happy or unhappy, creative or uninteresting, secure or lonely.

There is not a profession in the whole wide world that has as much freedom or as much time to be creative as that of a wife. If you doubt this, spend a morning in your local library going over the job descriptions and requirements and pay scales.

A wife needs to learn to like herself well enough to say, "I am a person. This is what I have chosen"—without feeling she has to defend *herself.*

When Husband starts trying to make over or change Wife, Wife's initial response is like that of Jo when she said, "Who does he think he is?" and rebellion sets in. When *she* sees something that she would like to change, she can do it for *herself* without resenting the change. To change is a choice.

Circumstances are not in charge. We may not have control over the circumstances around us but neither do the circumstances have control of us.

Judy shared with me how, in sixteen years of marriage, each year at the family reunion there was a digging back into the past. The "excavation" brought up every bad thing that had happened with a placing of blame on different members of the family who were usually not present. During this time each year she would come away almost ill because of all the criticism. This past year *she decided* not to be a part of this discussion. Rather, she chose to move around and share in the groups that were positive. When she could no longer find anyone to share with she moved into the backyard and sat alone. In only a short time she was joined by another member of the family who asked why she was outside. Judy replied that she did not wish to participate in tearing a family member apart. Judy said to me, "I came away for the first time in all these years feeling good about myself because I had chosen what I wanted to do."

There may be an unhappy atmosphere around a wife but she can decide for herself to be happy. A wife *holds the key to her own happiness.*

Self-confidence is a grand thing if you possess it; an ugly monster if it possesses you. The choice is ours to reject, tolerate, or accept *self* as we are today. The choice we make for *self* will determine the measure we use on our husband, children, and friends.

Rejection leaves nothing to work with. Toleration only lasts for a limited time. Acceptance is the sure road to success in *liking self* and in building a good marriage relationship.

Everyone likes the place of importance which puts them in charge of others, but few people realize there is nothing quite as fulfilling as being in charge of *self.*

Your Marriage As You See It

3
Your Marriage As You See It

"Help me out of this marriage. There is not one reason for our staying together. I don't even like him anymore." This was a tearful plea from Janice, in her late twenties. But she looked forty because of the emotional anxiety she had put herself through, as she had recanted all of the failures that were evident in her marriage relationship.

A true picture of the marriage must be painted before one can tell what virtues the marriage has. This is difficult to do if you only look at what is wrong with a marriage. An eye-opening experience is to draw a picture or make a collage of what your marriage looks like to you. Then you can sit back and take a long look at what is right and needs strengthening and what is wrong and needs changing.

Following this suggestion Janice was amazed at all of the good things in her marriage. She was really pleased but explained, "They are still not all that I want them to be."

The majority of the wives I know are just letting marriage "happen" to them. The whole relationship seems to be out of control and not at all what they want. There seems to be more of the *for worse* experiences than the *for better* experiences that they had dreamed would happen.

Freedom desired. "If I could just do what I want to do for a change"—a common remark in most group discussions. Freedom sought by a wife many times is defined as a relief from being responsible to anyone—especially her husband.

Which freedom is she asking for: freedom of speech, freedom from want, freedom of will, exemption of responsibility, or liberation from sharing with her husband? The identity crisis of a wife

47

cannot be solved separate from her marriage relationship unless she chooses to be alone, and in that case she is no longer classified as a wife.

The main restraint or bondage a woman must be liberated from is the idea that she must let someone else read *her sealed orders to her and interpret them for her.*

Freedom in marriage is *not independence.* Marriage means she has chosen to build a life with a husband, not separate from a husband. Emotional divorce can become painfully real in husband-wife relationships. They are married in name only. They go their separate ways and refuse to blend their lives together. This is one of the major causes for loneliness in life. There must be a sharing of who she is and what she wants—even if it means "making waves." Otherwise there will be nothing more than an empty, wasted feeling of merely existing.

Nora painted a graphic picture of freedom in marriage as she talked about the success of her husband and the great career she had made for herself. She shared, with a bit of loneliness in her voice, how her three children were now married and moved away. Then she began to cry as she told me her husband had said to her, "I want a divorce."

"I planned since the children were small for this time with my husband when we would be financially secure and free to do whatever we wanted to do," she sobbed. When I asked if the planning had been done with her husband her reply was, "No, I just thought we both were working toward the same goals."

There is more than enough freedom for deciding who she wants to spend her life with and for working together to accomplish the kind of relationship they both desire.

A wife is free to decide if it will be: until death do us part or living death; bonding together or picking apart; looking at what is right or only at what is wrong; caring enough to try or calling it a failure; contributing to a better relationship or blaming her husband for the entire mess.

It is hard to build a relationship with a man. Whether secluded on a ranch in Arizona or in Metropolitan Los Angeles, a wife is still dealing on a one-to-one basis as wife to her husband.

Difficult as it may be to work toward a good marriage, some still succeed. Two special people I know have been married 62 years. They provide an excellent example that it is possible to have a good marriage. As I observe them in their day-to-day life I see two distinct individuals working together to enjoy a good relationship. They have redefined their contributions to each other many times through the years.

Every woman wants to be free and *is* free to discover her own identity in marriage.

For better or for worse, for richer or for poorer, in sickness and in health. Let's "accentuate the positive." There are happy areas in even the most unpleasant of marriages. These are the areas that would be included if a wife were trying to tell a young woman what makes a good marriage.

Her picture would include the *contributions* she makes to the marriage that give her satisfaction and fulfillment as a person in the capacity of wife. This must include the areas that she enjoys because they give her room to grow as an individual.

Life is more worthwhile when even a small part of the fairy tale that says, "They lived happily ever after," has come true. Experiences that are particularly meaningful to a wife and make her feel alive and happy to be in this marriage with her husband need expression.

The song that goes, "You've gotta have a dream if you want a dream to come true," is a good place to begin. The happy ideas that a young woman brings to marriage can be put into practice anytime she chooses. The things she wants to contribute and can contribute—things that would be constructive to the relationship— should be the starting place for making a better marriage.

What made the thought of life together so enjoyable? Is this impossible now? Does the bride think only of the things that will be done *for* her?

When discussing her readiness for marriage, Dawn enthusiastically said, "I feel I am ready for marriage. I am not marrying John so I can be happy. I just want to be with him and share my happiness." She was coming to marriage with more maturity than most women gain in a lifetime.

The more a wife puts into the relationship, the happier she will be about the relationship.

"Eliminate the negative." One of the primary causes for the fall of Germany in World War II was the refusal of Hitler to hear any reports that were negative.

There is no such thing as a *perfect* marriage, so there is room for improvement in every marriage. Some wives think the easiest place to bring about these necessary improvements is in the area of the husband's responsibilities.

Where does unhappiness in marriage come from? Is it delivered by a big, bad man in grotesque make-up? Or is the wife just one of those unlucky people who has only wrong things *happening* to her?

In marriage someone has to take the blame if things are going badly. It is extremely easy for a wife to see what is wrong—*her husband,* of course! There are those things that *he is not* doing that are a requirement for *her* happiness. Then again, there are those things *he is* doing that hinder *her* happiness.

I simply must ask, "By whose standard? By mutual agreement? Who made her the final authority on what *he* should do or not do?" The wife who is on this bent must ask herself a question. If I have a better plan that would bring more happiness into the marriage, why haven't I shared this big, wonderful plan with the man of my dreams?

If God allowed a wife the privilege, that God himself does not even use, of changing her husband, would she be happy then? I say, "No." In the first place many women operate on what they *feel* about things more than the *facts* and what must be done. If a woman had the power to change her husband, she might be in a different mood tomorrow and want something else, and the poor husband would be torn apart in the constant change.

There are three major hindrances to a good relationship in marriage. All three hindrances are ones that she can do something about and are *not* controlled by the *other person.* These major destroyers are within her realm of correction. They are tension (which causes frustration), worry, and anger.

We have a robber in our midst and are failing to capture him if we are letting tension and frustration be intruders in our lives. We are robbed of happiness, joy, and health. Who can have happiness and enjoy life when he is uptight all of the time? (Dr. S. I. McMillen has written a beautiful book, *None Of These Diseases*, explaining how much the tensions in our bodies impair our health.)

One cause of tension in our lives is trying to live someone else's life in preference to our own. Carol came storming into class quite obviously very upset. "What has happened to you?" Joy asked as she tried to calm Carol down. "A stupid driver just stopped right in front of me and I nearly hit him, and I had my car full of children, and I was late getting off this morning, and my husband got up in a grouchy mood and was upset because he didn't have a clean shirt and, and . . ." Carol burst into tears. Trying to get everyone around her to fit her schedule, and planning her schedule as she goes without saying a word except in frustration, will always end in defeat and exasperation.

Another cause of tension is being angry with self because we have not performed perfectly. What is wrong with a wife who, when her husband is five minutes late, screams, "Why are you always late for dinner just when I have something planned?"?

She probably has had a day in which she has not controlled her time well. She has more than likely not accomplished all that she had wanted to and is running behind her vague schedule. So she attacks him instead of admitting where she is in her own schedule. It is temptingly easier that way. Tension and frustration are too heavy to carry, along with all you have planned to do today. Assuming someone else is to blame for your unhappiness gives the feeling that "everyone is after me—poor me!"

One morning I was in a rush to get my hair dry, so I could make it to class. I jerked the hair dryer out of the closet and plugged it in; then set out to search for the hood. I looked in each of my daughters' rooms, under their beds, in the bathrooms, in the closet, and became more frustrated as my time ticked away. In my desperation, with quite a lecture to each of the girls going on in my mind, I decided to look in the end of the dryer where the cap belongs—and, lo and behold, it was there. I had assumed that they hadn't put it up this time, either, and had wasted ten precious minutes operating on that basis.

Trying to control, blame, or assume someone else has done something will always bring you tension and frustration if that is what you want.

Another hindrance to building a good relationship is worry. Worry is totally unnecessary and unproductive in our lives. Most women kid themselves into putting a *concern* label on *worry*. Concern is planning to correct or helping to correct something that is wrong. If there is nothing you can do about what is wrong, then it is not your assignment. Any time you spend trying to predict what might go wrong is only robbing you of precious time and energy.

Worrying for fear your child may fall off of the swing at school and break his leg. Worrying for fear your teenager may have an accident in the car.

What can you do in either case? You can teach and train your children how to make correct choices in their lives and then let them go to live their own lives.

A poem a friend shared with me expresses it well:

> I worry, I putter, I push, I shove
> Hunting little mole hills
> To make mountains of.

Worry is one of life's biggest wastes. You can do all of your ironing or cleaning or whatever you have to do with the energy you spend worrying. God says if we will take care of our assignments today, he will take care of our tomorrows which, by the way, are his assignment.

The third culprit that does untold damage to marriage is anger. In Christian circles we often teach that to control your anger is virtuous. Jesus' very words to us were not to control, but to *deal* with anger today. When anger is not dealt with it is simply stored away in the form of resentment only to rear its ugly head at a later date.

Decide today to become a "sweet little old lady" that is a delightful person to be around. What is done today lasts forever. If anger is not dealt with it becomes resentment. This takes place when there is a failure to be honest and communicate feelings and thinking about self. Resentment turns to bitterness. A little bitterness multiplies and eventually a person becomes a hateful, cutting, ugly, cruel individual, a person everyone dreads to encounter.

Permission granted to take advantage. Lest I paint an impossible picture of building a good marriage, let me hasten to explain: there is something each wife can do to build a better relationship with her husband.

A good place to begin is to enjoy what is good in her marriage. Look at the picture of your marriage that you drew at the beginning of this chapter. Check to see if you didn't put at least one thing you feel *is just right*. Major on that good point. Choose to reflect on it throughout the day. You have to spend your time thinking about something because your mind is never idle. *Think* about what is good in your marriage.

Where to begin change? After finding a number, even if the number is one, of things that you do not wish to change, you are ready to get down to business with building a better marriage. There must be a selection of the particular change that needs to be made. Is there anything you can do about it? If not, you must select another that you can change. This necessitates that it be something regarding *you* since you are *only* in control of yourself.

Rebellion sets in when change is considered. My beautician tells me that my hair takes two or three weeks to settle down and start responding when I change from one style to another. Some of the rebellion sounds like what June said when I introduced the idea of a wife's part in changing the marriage. "Why should I have to do all of the changing? Isn't this a marriage of two people? What is *he* supposed to do?"

True, it is a marriage of two people and the husband has some responsibilities that he must perform if the marriage is to be all

that it should be. *But* that is not the side of the marriage on which
she is standing. As a wife she can only work from the wife's vantage
point. Doing something about the change she wants to make should
be done today.

The desire for change is the place of beginning. A plan of *how*
to change must be drawn up by the person desiring to change.
I am a lousy letter writer, because all I have is a desire to communicate with my friends. I only do something about it when I
decide I am going to write, get the materials together, and write.
I have never contacted a friend by just talking about it or wanting
to do it.

Struggle is a necessary part of accomplishment. Abraham Lincoln
said, "When you resolutely decide to do something, fifty per cent
of your battle is won." The other fifty per cent is added as it is
done. Change calls for self-evaluation, time, patience, repetition,
and being willing to fail and try again.

At times all of us have that feeling of being out of control of
the world around us. It is a desperate feeling which comes over
us as we see things happening, things we would like to see different
from what they are—and we have no power to change them.

It is hopeless desperation if we are going to attempt a remedy
of the problem from the other person's standpoint. The only control
that we have in world affairs is determined by the beginning
of change within us. Being in charge of the situation has to begin
with being in control of oneself. What I do or do not do today
will affect the rest of my life.

Speak up! Back to the picture. There you see something he is
doing or needs to do that in your opinion would be helpful to
your relationship. Talk—or maybe I should say "communicate"—with him about it. He has told you before that he is not
a mind reader. The reason I suggest "communication" is because
that involves listening, as well as telling. If you plan on *telling*
him what *he* needs to change you may as well *forget it*. It has
not worked before, it will not work this time, or the next one
hundred times. Remember what you really need to express is
what your needs are, and not what he should do about your needs.

Telling him what he should do about your needs is like running to the other side of the net after you have served the ball and telling the other tennis player how to return it to you. You will spend all of your life telling and never be in your place to receive unless you stay on your side of the marriage.

Seeing Husband As He Is

4
Seeing Husband As He Is

Building a life together requires knowing who you are as a wife and understanding who he is as a husband.

Many times an excited bride-to-be has written long letters extolling the excellent qualities of the future bridegroom. They tell how handsome, thoughtful, outgoing, kind, strong, respectful, humorous, well traveled, considerate, affectionate, mature, clean, independent, family oriented, sensitive, intelligent, interesting, dependable, ingenious, athletic, and sexy he is.

This husband-to-be is just too good to be true. He is exactly as she dreamed he would be. All of those good qualities drew her to him. They were so obvious to her. Since they were discernible to her she couldn't understand how anyone could find anything to criticize him about. Like the daughters in "Fiddler on the Roof," as they expressed their desire to be married, she said if the matchmaker found someone for her she "would be the envy of all." Then after a sudden pang of thought, "I could get stuck for good."

"What you see is what you get." From number one admirer to number one critic in one, single marriage ceremony. From handsome to conceited; thoughtful to unappreciative; outgoing to gabby; kind to inconsiderate; strong to a bully; respectful to disrespectful, humorous to a bore; well traveled to gad-about; considerate to selfish; affectionate to over-sexed; mature to needing supervision; clean to *Mr. Clean;* independent to dictator; sensitive to insensitive; intelligent to know-it-all; athletic to sports fanatic.

What happened? The change was made if and when she decided to major on negatives instead of positives. No one admits to deciding—it just happens. Does it? It happens when judgment is made and the remodeling begun. It happens when no consideration is given to the fact that men and women are different. It happens when she uses her background as a measure for his conduct. It happens when she sets herself up as the final authority, infallible.

In order to assess your husband correctly you will want to spend some time on what his accomplishments were before he met you—all of those exciting "youth" kind of accomplishments which are so important to him and are stored securely in his memory bank. Among these are numbered scholastic accomplishments, athletic victories, monetary endeavors, and whatever you do, you must not leave out his desirability to the opposite sex.

Before marriage you were free with your compliments, saw his potential, and were excited about what he would become.

Some thought questions that might be of value:

How many of these qualities does he still possess?

How many of them do you still enjoy?

How long has it been since you thought about these things?

Take a further look at those things you have shared with him in planning and seen accomplished, like your wedding, your first home together, vacations, entertaining friends, changing jobs, starting a family.

Have you expressed appreciation to him for the privilege of sharing his life with him thus far?

There is more to come! The dreams he has shared with you, "When we can afford it we will . . . go to Hawaii, buy a boat, buy a house, send our children to college, go into business . . ." or whatever particular flavor his dreams take.

Keep adventure in life. You need to keep discovering more about your husband. You will never exhaust all of the facets to your man.

For a wife to see her husband as he *is*, she needs to major on what he brought to the marriage. One thing she knows for sure is that he has good judgment concerning women! Out of all of the girls he dated, he chose her. This proves the man's good taste and intelligence. He asked her to blend her life with his in a *lifetime commitment.* The asking and the accepting are really an agreement between the two to become a part of the other. The Scriptures express it as leaving every other person in your life and making *each other first*. It is a bonding together of two unique individuals with God's glue. The two become *one* and *number one* with each other—twice as strong, two opinions in order to reach one conclusion.

The becoming *one* is a lifetime process. Do not interpret this to mean that all others are cut out of his or her life and the two are destined to survive alone in isolation. Rather, it means that each is to place the other in the category of first consideration above all others. One reason this is necessary, in order to build a strong marriage relationship, is that everything each partner does affects the other one. This is not to indicate that the wife and husband must travel the same path and do everything together in order to build a good marriage. It does mean that as each grows or refuses to grow in the relationship, the other is built up or torn down by that decision.

The marriage contract has both husband and wife pledging to work at the relationship for a lifetime. This should mean security to both and a commitment to do her part as the wife. In addition to a lifetime commitment he came to marriage planning to contribute *a male point of view, a plan of finance, and leadership.*

A husband has a tremendous assignment from God. He may not be trained for the role of husband but he must shoulder responsibility for which he is not given credit in a large number of cases.

He has not been taught what his responsibilities are in marriage, except by the joking of other men and the pattern of his parents. A few days before their divorce was final, Tom and Lois decided to try one more time to straighten out their marriage. Tom said to me, "I have no earthly idea what is required of me in order to have a happy marriage. In fact, until I realized we were destroying what I wanted most I hadn't given a thought to my role beyond finances and sex." The happy ending to this story is: when Tom was given guidance in how to find the magic ingredients to happy marriage, he and Lois began working together and finding answers that are acceptable to both.

◄ I hope that we never get the matter of equal rights confused to the extent we are striving for *alikeness*. If we were alike there would be no addition to the blending of two lives. It would just be some more of the same. The Scriptures tell us that God made *male* and *female* both in his image, both with assignments to carry out, both with a need for the other. Part of the problem in defining roles and finding identity is in the area of fear about not being as important as the other person in the marriage.

Do not let today's vocal few confuse the issue for you. Let the remarriage rate in our country today tell you something about the need to belong to and share with the man of your choosing. A marriage dissolution is hardly final until both parties are seeking someone else with which to begin building a relationship and the wife still has to work from her side.

A male point of view is a nice thing to have. I never cease to be amazed at the wives who are disturbed in the marriage relationship because their husbands do not see things the way they see them; do not feel like they do about things that are very important to them; and feel that they do not love them because they differ with them in so many vital areas.

God does not intend that husband and wife be *natural enemies*. We are supposed to have joined forces to be constructive, not to destroy one another. The building begins to be real when we are thankful for a different point of view, instead of threatened and defensive when that view is stated.

The pattern that was set in her own home by her mother and father either helps or hinders the acceptance of her husband's point of view.

A plan of finance was the topic of a small sharing group that was started by Joyce's commenting, "In my family we always . . ." and the group froze in place. The phrase "we always" is hard to communicate beyond because the thoughts begin racing, "What a mess her family is, anyway, or we don't want to be like that family."

Both wife and husband bring to the marriage their ideas about how the finances should be handled. They either come thinking there is just *no other way* or saying *we do not want* to make the same mistakes our parents made. Even though it may have been very right for their parents or very wrong for them, the fact still remains that the two must work together in formulating *their own plan.*

"You must be kidding," Joyce, laughing insecurely, said. "You don't know what a sorry manager my husband is with money. He can't hold onto the stuff long enough to get the bills paid." I did not say the husband comes as a financial wizard to this marriage. He comes with his own ideas, which are valid, and require being heard if the two are to build a successful financial program.

Leadership! "Follow the leader" is a fun game when the leader is creative and considerate. The game ceases to be when each player tries to become the leader.

We follow this design of one leader in business, but it becomes unacceptable when we come to marriage. A business cannot survive and thrive when it does not have a leader. If two equal partners own a business and a disagreement comes up that cannot be settled between the two of them, the court must step in and dissolve the partnership. When husband and wife stand toe to toe and eye to eye with differing opinions and convictions, one of two things must happen. Either one backs off and yields to the other's plan, or there is a dissolution of the marriage.

God is interested in every person having a happy marriage, so he designed the pattern to make that possible. The design is that the *husband* is to be the leader in the home and responsible directly to God. The *wife* is to be a *participating follower* knowing that she is obedient to God when she is following her husband.

The Los Angeles zoo has a two-headed snake which was pictured in a local paper. The snake has more of a problem than just having two heads. It has the complication of moving to any given destination, because it is headed in two directions, and thus cannot move without one head overpowering the other and dragging it along. This is a graphic picture of the majority of marriages.

A fifty-fifty basis says no controlling interest and causes lack of leadership, lack of support, and lack of security. Even a fifty-one—forty-nine would be a help.

A supported leader, from a sense of fairness, feels a deep desire to give complete consideration to the subject at hand.

⌁ The greatest gift that a husband and wife give to their children is loving each other. When there is love shared between the parents there is security for the children. The child can be trained, taught, and prepared for a steady growth with good patterns that are difficult to learn outside the home.

Being a father is a secondary role that man carries to the marriage. He is *husband first* and needs to be assured of the importance of this role to his wife. So he brought all of this to the marriage; what does he hope to get? He is looking for total commitment⌁ to him. *All of her.* One of the reasons we are willing to make lifetime commitments to each other is our need to ask the total involvement of each other's life. This is not to say we must be like a turtle and his shell, never parting company. It is the support of each to the other that is so vital. Knowing that neither would do anything to harm the other intentionally is a comfort.

⌁ The husband wants his wife to be happy. One of the most common statements husbands make is, "I just want her to be happy." He does much of what he does in trying to accomplish her happiness, not realizing that he is *not* responsible for her happiness. *That is her own assignment.*

He wants a wife who will contribute *her* part. Today, a sure way to get a heated discussion going is to mention the woman's *role.* We are a non-classification society with a *don't-put-me-in-a-slot* complex. Relax. I do not intend to spell this out for you. The two must decide the plan of action. I am saying that this is a two-part contract and you have your side of it to fill. May I kindly suggest your marriage is a joint effort? If it is a struggle for equality, it will end up a tug-of-war where even the winner loses.

A wife needs to keep her eyes wide open to discover who her husband has become each day, so she will keep up the relationship. Adopting the attitude that *she knows* who he is because of past performance causes the familiar, "I am living with a complete stranger. I just don't know who he is anymore."

How a Wife Communicates
Her Needs

5
How a Wife Communicates Her Needs

"Not to communicate is to become alienated, to be unable to participate in another's life," according to D. H. Small in *After You've Said I Do.*

What is needed are instructions in *how* to communicate instead of being told that we need to communicate. In conversation with a communications expert I said, "One of the biggest helps to building a better marriage would be to be able to communicate." The expert's reply was, "My wife and I do not have any problems in communication." "Excellent. What do you communicate about?" I asked. Thoughtful silence—"We talk about the children. When the house needs painting . . . I see what you mean. We need to learn about each other."

Communication is dialogue. Who is capable of dialogue? Howe says in *The Miracle of Dialogue:*

He is one who responds to others with his whole being and not with just a part of himself, and he is able to listen with his heart as well as with his mind. He is really present; he does not run off on "errands" while he seems to be listening to the person before him. He is an authentic person, too, in the sense that he is able to learn as well as to teach, to accept love as well as to love, to be ministered unto as well as to minister.[1]

A wife will participate in her husband's life as she shares who she is *today* and seeks equally to know who he is *today.* As she seeks to find more about who he is and what he likes and dislikes, she becomes more involved with him as a person.

"My husband just will not talk to me. All he ever wants to do is sit in front of that dumb television," Emily said angrily. When

I asked Emily what she wanted to communicate, she said, "I just want to tell him what I think about the way things are going in our marriage." What I heard Emily saying was that she wanted to *tell* her husband what a rotten husband he was being and what he should be doing to please her. And label that communication!

The problem of not being able to get through to the other person could be caused by the *non-verbal* communication that is being heard loud and clear. When our words and our body language are in conflict we are heard to be saying *No* but *Yes.*

Since most men are body watchers it is only natural that communication by body language comes across first. The turning of the head, the cut of the eyes, the expression of the mouth all give the first signals of the opinion that wishes to be communicated from inside the person.

James was feverishly expressing his ideas one evening in a group when his wife, Louise, quietly laid her hand on his leg, and the conversation stopped as abruptly as if a tape recorder had been turned off. They exchanged *looks* and then she said, "Go ahead," but that was the end of the dissertation. Louise could not have been more definite in her communication had she stood to her feet and screamed, "Shut up, you fool!"

It is sad that most people feel that communication is *telling another what THEY should do.*

There are many levels of communication that we engage in each day. The one most needed between wife and husband is about the things she likes concerning who she is, what she thinks, what she feels, and what she wants to do about her wants. When she talks about what she plans to do about her needs, she is *hitting the ball when it is served to her on her side of the court.*

There are several ways that this can be done. Begin first with body language. This is where the message—given verbally, written, or by doing things that share herself—is verified or denied.

Some wives have kept quiet so long for the sake of the marriage or children or family that they do not know how to make a positive statement about things they are pleased with in their lives. Sometimes a good place to begin is by *writing notes.* Leaving a note, saying where she is when her husband is likely to return home first, helps. If he is a "brown bagger," a kind word with his peanut butter sandwich will make it more delicious. If he is a traveling man, a note in his sox or attached to his toothbrush gets the message across. Writing can never be a substitute for oral communication, but it can be a beginning and an enhancer.

All means—body language, oral, written, and doing—must be sending the same signals of who she is, what she thinks, how she feels, and what she is doing about herself. An inconsistent message is confusing to the recipient and usually ignored.

Sharing herself caused Sue to say, "I have come off a negative kick and I feel so good about me. I was in charge of me today and I accomplished so much."

A husband is being asked to do an impossible task when he is asked to make his wife happy. When a wife assumes responsibility for her own happiness, she needs to communicate the information to her husband. "Not me. If I do that he will not listen to anything that I have to say about what is wrong again." That was Rosa's comment about sharing where she was trying to improve communication from her side of the marriage.

The fact is that when a wife is feeding only negatives, her husband is letting it go in one ear and out the other without registering acknowledgment. We do not mind hearing negative responses if they are not all of the communication there is.

When she chooses to share the good side of herself and look at the "pluses" in her marriage, she encourages her husband and finds motivation for herself.

Communicating gives the warmth and feeling of belonging that most of us desire in marriage.

"But I am not all positives. I have many areas in my life that I need to share with my husband that are hurting areas and need his attention. How do I communicate them so he can hear me?" Good question, Debbie.

Happiness, joy, exuberance, love, sorrow, fear, worry, anger are all part of our lives. To be without emotions is to be ill. Emotions are what put the spark in our living.

On the other hand, to be ruled over by our emotions is a disaster. How can something so good be so bad? Emotion becomes our ruin when it is not disciplined. When our feelings at the moment control the whole of life, instead of being controlled as an important part of life, we are in trouble. This is expressed by *I don't feel like doing what I am responsible for today.* A life guided by feelings alone is destined to be in upheaval most of the time. Running on emotion instead of by choice is an uphill journey all the way.

The best time to begin in communication is when we are in control. Learn to verbalize the happiness, joy, and love that is there. We feel these emotions but rarely stop to identify what has caused these responses and who or what has been responsible.

Most people wait for the ones around them to bring these emotions out. The truth is emotions are controlled from within. The wife who is happy has chosen to accept what is going on around her and looks at the things that please her instead of the things that displease her. She looks at the *have's* instead of the *have not's.*

The emotions of fear, worry, and anger are ones that we must learn to *deal* with because they are a part of our everyday lives.

Fear comes mainly from a lack of confidence in God and in self. A growing relationship to God gives us confidence that He is willing to direct our paths, and to keep His eye on us. Since He wants us to be happy and to have only the best we must learn to accept this for ourselves. Fear is a form of emotional "atheism" because it says God is not able to do what he promises.

Worry is totally unnecessary for believers who claim Matthew 6:31-34 as their promise. We need to relate our lives to God, and he will provide for us today and take care of us tomorrow when it gets here. Our side of the promise is to relate our lives to him and use what he gives us and his side is to provide; hence *no* worry. We work on our assignments and allow God to work on his. What accident is it possible for us to prevent by worrying about it?

We place a *concern* label on worry in order to justify our anxiety. Concern is thinking about something and planning what we can do about it and putting our plans into action. If there is nothing we can do about it, it needs to be committed to God and put out of our thinking because it only saps us of much needed strength that we can use in an area of meeting needs either for ourselves or others. Valuable time is wasted in worry.

We recognize fear and worry as things we do to ourselves, but we usually think of anger as something toward others. The most harm done in anger is done to the angry person. Anger is a difficult emotion with which to work. The "count to ten" or "go for a walk" or "forget" it, or whatever method is used, must be questioned to see if the anger is being dealt with or if it is taking over.

I think we have misunderstood the Bible when it says, "Be ye angry and sin not," to mean that we should *contain* ourselves and *maintain* as if we were not in a state of displeasure or hurt. Anger is as much a part of our make-up as hunger when we have not eaten for a long period of time. The other half of the verse says, "Let not the sun go down upon your wrath." In other words, anger can't wait—it must be dealt with *now*. (cf. Eph. 4:26)

Another important fact we fail to consider is that we have a limited capacity for storing anger. Today's anger becomes tomorrow's resentments. And resentment is there to stay until something is done with it or it does something with us. Resentment aged becomes bitterness. When we become angry our body chemistry actually changes.

Dr. Rubin in *The Angry Book* lists over thirty ways we pervert anger and twist it around. He shows how it becomes poison to our systems.

When anger is not dealt with, it is stored, whether we acknowledge the storage or not. It will not go away on its own but settles in the back of the mind to be acted on at a later date. Each person has a limited space for storing resentment before it forces its way out into action.

Those actions may be in the form of an explosion, silence, or nothingness. These are safety valves to keep from killing someone else, destroying oneself or "flipping out" (losing touch with reality).

The wife who screams at her children for seemingly no reason at all or berates her husband for being five minutes late needs to recognize that she is *boiling over* because she has reached capacity in the storage of resentments.

With some the explosion is loud and boisterous, while with others it is quieter and more subdued, but nevertheless vented. With all of the words, the matter is not dealt with unless a person comes to a satisfactory solution. Just talking about it will not suffice.

Silence in a relationship says a person has moved away emotionally. This is said to be the cruelest treatment one person can give to another. It is meant to be. It is saying basically, "You crumb, you don't even deserve to hear my high and lofty thoughts." The communication is, "I do not care about you."

Another result of unexpressed anger is the passive role of acting as if a person does not care. Forget it! This is a numb state in which she is present physically but refuses to be open for fear of being hurt. Hurt is another way of saying, "I am angry." Anything that is said to her calls for no response because she cannot put part of her emotions in the freezer and leave the others out to thaw. When she stores them away, so she cannot be *hurt*, she also has them put away so she cannot enjoy the happiness and love around her.

"So I read you. It is dangerous to store up resentment so I must learn to express myself. Where do I begin?" This is often said to me.

Honesty is the best policy. You must face what the real cause of your displeasure is. Are you angry with yourself because you have not performed to your satisfaction? Are you trying to live someone else's life for them? Are you trying to tell others what they should be doing to make you happy?

Three blocks that are destructive in dealing with anger:

1) The attitude that it is not nice to be angry. Assuming responsibility for keeping life running on a smooth, even keel. Saying, "Everything is beautiful" regardless of how you are hurting.

2) The common belief that self-control at any price is the Christian thing to do. Self-control is helpful while one is deciding how to deal with anger. Acting as if it never happened or thinking

a person got what he deserved or intending to take care of it later are all ways of storing up resentments that will eventually have to be dealt with.

3) The aloofness of "mind your own business." This is the way we say, "Don't touch me or don't ask me to become involved."

Stored anger becomes the "uglies" in life. Resentment becomes bitterness which causes anxiety, depression, guilt, thoughtlessness, that always tired feeling (fatigue), psychosomatic illness, constant temper tantrums, and many other undesirables in one's life.

Dealing with anger necessitates being in control of yourself, but not trying to control someone else. One of the heaviest resentment builders is the anger we experience because of the way others choose to live their lives. Dealing with anger means feeling with all of your feelings and allowing your husband the same privilege. It means expressing your feelings of displeasure from the point of how it affects you and not in a judgmental *you should* attitude.

The only way I have ever seen resentment adequately brought out of storage is to forgive the person who has been responsible for the hurting. Asking forgiveness of her husband for the part she had in the argument is doing all she can do to begin dealing. When there has been a disagreement each one has had a part. Some women feel that they are not a party to the argument if they are passive, but this is not so. To me, the turning of the other cheek that Jesus taught is the way to a solution. This means that we should be willing to go beyond seeing who could strike the last blow—not to strike back and to agree there is a solution that is acceptable to both husband and wife starts the repairs.

The wife needs to ask forgiveness for what she has done wrong. It is a much easier solution to deal with the anger today by looking honestly at the cause of her anger. Is it legitimate? By that I mean is there something that she can do about it in her own life? If not, she decides that if she cannot change it, it is not her problem and she asks God to forgive her for judging her husband.

When trying to decide where to begin in the removal of stored up resentment a good question is, "What is bugging you most?" When you have decided on *one* thing, you must ask yourself, "What

can I do about it?" The acceptable way to handle the problem
is to say that you are sorry. "Sorry for what?" he will ask. You
then must deal with specifics.

I'm sorry calls for no response from the husband. When you
ask for forgiveness for a specific thing, then it is the husband's
move to respond. He has the choice to respond any way he wants
to. He may ignore you. He may say that there was nothing to
it. He may say he didn't notice or does not know what you are
talking about. He may say he is not ready to forgive you or that
he cannot forgive you. His response is *his to decide* and to live
with. Yours is for you to work with and build the relationship
by contributing what you know is right. This should not be done
on the basis of what he decided he will do in responding. You
cannot prevent him from storing resentments if that is what he
chooses. You must continue to work in your own life.

Do not ask God to do your forgiving for you. Do your *own*
forgiving. God forgives us after we ask and when we have been
in disagreement with him and decide that he is right and we are
wrong. God tells us that when we are dealing with others, we are
to do the forgiving and asking for forgiveness. He says that we
cannot really understand what forgiveness is all about until we
have worked with it on a basis with other people. The number
one area where this ought to be practiced is in the husband/wife
relationship.

"I am not about to ask forgiveness when I am right and he
is wrong. How mixed up can a person get?" was Eileen's angry
comment to me. I tried to help her see her part in beginning to
work through the problem between her and her husband. Forgiveness has a restoring quality in any relationship. It puts us on a
basis of a new beginning with each other.

When trying to communicate, we receive about as much attention
as we are willing to give. A wife has the choice of responding
to her husband or reacting to him. Response must be learned.
Reaction is natural. We hear what we expect to hear and we stop
listening when we hear key words. Words like bossy, nagging, poor
manager, always late, submission, obey, "you are *just* like your

mother." An immediate reaction sets in and we speak too soon, say too much, and have too little understanding of what the other person is trying to communicate. My friend Jane put it like this, "The only exercise my husband ever enjoys is jumping to conclusions." When we become defensive, we are more concerned about our own needs and are *judging, not listening,* to the other person.

Response cannot rightly be made until a wife first identifies herself and learns to like who she is as a wife. As a wife does this, she does not feel threatened from every side. This is also the basis for allowing her husband to be himself without her trying to change him.

The most important things a wife has to share with her husband are about herself. She is the only one that knows her real self. She has all of herself and she is developing her potential from day to day and changing her ideas. She is having new thoughts that must be shared with her husband if he is to really know who she is.

Margie said, "I am very confused. He knew what I needed and what made me happy before marriage. Why doesn't he know now?" Just because he accidentally hit on some of her "likes" before marriage does not make him responsible for living on a day-by-day guessing game basis all his life. She needs to tell him who she is, what she thinks, how she feels, what she wants, and what she needs. I am not suggesting that these all be done in one evening but as a day-to-day sharing.

Who is free to listen? Communication is only possible when two people give each other their presence. The listening that a wife does should be at least two-thirds of her communication. Listening helps her know who she is building the relationship with, what he needs, and what he is trying to contribute. *She is not listening until she has a greater desire to understand than to be understood.*

Specific questioning aids the beginning of sharing. Diane said, "I always call to my husband from wherever I am in the house and ask what he did today as soon as he comes in the door. He always says, 'The same old thing,' and that is the end of the conversation. I've tried. Believe me. I have really tried. He just does not want to talk to me."

We are off and communicating *only* when we have established that someone is listening. I suggested that Joyce try being present visibly and ask, "What was the most interesting thing you did today?" and then see what response she received. She returned the following week, saying, "I can't tell you how neat it is to have him share some of his life with me." He is motivated to tell her who he is when she is there (present).

When a husband starts sharing who he is and feels his wife cares enough about him to listen, it presents another problem. If she is not careful, she will find herself arguing about what his needs are. He is the one who knows what his needs are and is trying to state them. She needs to learn to ask questions when she does not understand, and then receive more information. She ought to stay with his thoughts and not jump ahead, *assuming* what he is going to say.

Understanding as you go is basic to communication. "Let's be totally honest with one another" sometimes means "Get ready to let me tell you exactly how *you* are." Personally, I stay clear of brutally frank people. They are usually saying, "I want to rip you apart and you have to listen and like it, because I am honest." It is important we understand that when we talk about being honest, we are talking about being honest about *ourselves*. *Self* is the person we know enough about to be sufficiently informed, and thus, to be honest.

A good exercise in understanding is to institute this rule. Each person can speak up for self only after she has first *restated* the *ideas* and *feelings* expressed by the *previous speaker accurately* and to the other person's satisfaction. This is responding. It keeps us from emotionally forming an evaluation from only our point of view.

Good communication cuts down on anger. Any judgment that is made should be about a wrongdoing and not judgment of the person. We want a responsive listener. Learn to express *yourself.* He may not like how you feel but he must know how you feel. No use? Yes, in the heat of the anger is where to begin work on the problem. Cool off. Ask for time to continue at a later hour *that day,* not another day. It will not seem as important tomorrow when it is stored neatly away in the resentment closet.

"It all sounds great when you say it in class, but it just doesn't work with my husband that way," Joan retorted. One of the reasons it did not work for Joan was the tone of voice, body language, and attitude she displayed. When she considered her *whole* message she was saying, "I'm giving you this information so you can straighten up." There are many ways to say, *"You should* do . . . because you are not acceptable to me as you are." The only hope Joan has is to return to her side of the court, where she can do something about the situation. As wife she needs to inventory the places that need some attention.

Don't hear me saying if something a husband does annoys her she is not supposed to say anything about it. She has every right—in fact, *must* tell him how she feels about what he is doing. But she has *no* right to tell him what to do about how she feels. There is no need for telling him more than once. He can hear. He is not deaf. If he continues as he was, he has not decided to make the change right now. He does not need, want, or appreciate her correction as if he were a child. He has outgrown the need for mothering.

The majority of the time we are aware of our mistakes and do not need to be told. The person who runs a red light on a left turn signal, and gets caught in the intersection with cars buzzing by on every side, does not need to be reminded by honking horns that he is in the wrong place. The communication he needs from his wife is not a lecture on driving safety, but on how frightened she was in that particular situation.

Most of the marital problems are worked and reworked to the point of frustration, but left unsolved because we are unwilling to go beyond the turbulence to solution. We would be awfully angry with an airline pilot who would stay in the storm instead of rising above it (when it was possible to have a smooth flight by his choosing to do so). We have the choice of moving on into the solution or staying where we are and enduring in tension and frustration until we are disgusted with the whole marriage affair. "Let's not talk about it anymore." These are worn-out words because we feel there is no ability to change the other person to our thinking—so, forget working on a better relationship in this area. As long as there is no solution that draws the two of you together, there is a wedge developing that will cause greater trouble later. In early marriage it is like a small splinter. As more resentments are added, because a suitable answer has not been found, the splinter becomes a wedge that drives husband and wife apart.

It is essential that husband and wife be able to work out satisfactorily anything that hinders a close feeling of being understood. She must insist on working beyond the explosion, tears, silence, or whatever, regardless of how difficult it may be, for the only way they can grow closer to each other is to deal with things that are coming between them. Since communication takes two, I want to re-emphasize that she is responsible *only* for the wife part but she is responsible for *all* of that.

Shelia was in tears as she spoke, "I try to share myself and tell my husband what I feel and what I think about things. He always says all I ever do is argue with him and I just don't feel that I am arguing. All I'm trying to do is express my opinion. I just can't get through to him."

We must look at how Shelia has approached the issue. Most of the time she asks him to tell her what he thinks about having the house painted. But when he tells her, she starts telling him what *she thinks* about painting the house. She needs to do her *telling* of what she thinks before asking for his decision. He really feels she is asking for a final decision because of how she approaches him, when all she wants is discussion. If discussion is what she wants, then she should begin by discussing from her point of view. When he brings it to a conclusion, discussion is cut off as far as he is concerned. Anything said further is questioning his decision. She must not ask for a judgment unless she has finished discussing it and is ready for the final decision to be made—and sometimes this may take days or weeks.

Communication does not kill healthy relationships, but it can be harmful to begin by emptying out all of the old resentments at one time—or by *telling the other person what is wrong with them and how they should act in response to you.*

Deal with your day-to-day anger (hurt or displeasure) by deciding if it needs to be expressed to your husband in order for you to be finished with it—or if you can make a judgment by yourself that it is your problem because of how you are trying to live his life.

Who says telling who you are and what you think must be in the negative case?

Marilyn asked, "What do you say when there is nothing positive to communicate? We are in the midst of legal proceedings over our business, and that is all I have to share."

"Is your husband employed?" I asked. "Well, yes, as a matter of fact, he has a very good business," was her reply. "Do you have a good relationship between you?" "Yes." "Do you have a nice house?" "Yes." "Health?" "Yes." "Friends?" "Yes." Then, with a bit of surprise in her voice, Marilyn said, "Really, the only thing wrong in our lives is the court proceedings and I see I have let it overshadow everything that is right. I have a place to begin."

In our own minds we all need to establish a positive place where we can begin to communicate.

---

[1] From *The Miracle of Dialogue* by Reuel Howe. Copyright 1963 by the Seabury Press, Inc. Used by permission of the publisher.

Wife's Need of Husband's Love

6
Wife's Need of Husband's Love

"What the world needs now is love, sweet love," is expressed
in the lyrics of a popular song. Everyone has the personal desire
to love and be loved. Each of us dreams in youth of what it would
be like to have someone love us enough to share his life with
us.

Love is one emotion that most people find a loss of words in
defining. It is said by some to be without definition. It is necessary
that we find what love means to us because our definition is spelled
out clearly by our attitudes and actions toward the one we claim
to love.

When I call for a defining of love in a group, regardless of age
or sex, there is the suggestion that there is no way to define it.

We say, "I love apple pie, I love to read, I love my children,
I love my husband." The word "love" has become common in
usage, but is not so common in experience. Most of the definitions
of love seem to say, "I get from you what I need and that brings
me enjoyment and pleasure."

One point of agreement is that loving and being loved are basic
needs of life. There have been numerous experiments of cutting
animals off from their group. It has been found that all of their
functions dwindle or are not as readily developed as when in the
atmosphere of care and attention. How much more is there a hunger
in all of us to be loved.

"I fell in love the summer of '52 or '62 or '72." By this we
are saying love slipped up and grabbed us without any choice
on our part. This means love is an uncontrollable emotion that
we hope happens to us.

How did she fall in love? Carla, a flirtatious eighteen-year-old said, "I just love Tom's personality, Dick's physique, Don's good looks, and Mark's spiritual qualities. When I find one guy with all of these assets put together, then I have found the man of my dreams." So she meets "Mr. Wonderful" all in one package and she says to me, "It was love at first glance!" Was it? She was looking for a number of attributes in a young man until she found him.

We do not want to stop our feelings. There is a legitimate sparkle and tingle in love before and after marriage. The danger is to let even a good emotion like love control our lives when it is defined as enjoyment another brings to us.

Coming to marriage, looking at only what is to be received from him to satisfy her, is what kills the beautiful beginning relationship in a few weeks. Familiarity truly does breed contempt unless the wife comes contributing her love as a gift to him, not seeking satisfaction from his love alone.

I heard a forlorn voice singing on the radio, "They just don't make love like they used to. It just seems to fall apart no matter what we do."

What is love made of? To find the ingredients, we must go to the maker. A product is best constructed or repaired by the manufacturer because he knows how it is designed and how it operates best. God has done something special for us. He loves us and wants every wife to have all the love she needs. He gave her a mind, temperament, talent, and a will all her own. He also gave her guidelines for feeling loved.

Scripture in the King James version uses the word "charity" in 1 Corinthians 13. When we think of charity we sometimes think of giving clothing, food, housing, or money to someone who has a physical need. We give something we have to them because they have a need for it at that particular time.

Physical need is only a part of the need in our lives. There are emotional, mental, and spiritual needs, also. *A need to be loved.*

Love is not automatic. Titus in the New Testament instructs the older women to *teach* the younger women to be wise and to *learn* to love their husbands and their children. Part of that teaching is given as she looks at God's love for her. She does not deserve His love and she will never be able to return it in full measure, but God keeps giving love to her.

The characteristics of God's perfect love are spelled out in 1 Corinthians 13:4-7. Here is a guide sheet for you to follow in *learning to love* yourself and your husband.

LOVE:
   Is patient in all kinds of situations.
   What does it mean? There is no problem being patient as long as everyone around is doing what we want them to do. One of the biggest causes of impatience is trying to control others. She is impatient with herself when she has not performed perfectly. She needs to give herself room to grow a step at a time. Patience can be gained when she spends time making the most out of her own life, while giving her husband the same privilege.
   Is kind regardless of how others act.
   Kindness seems to be hardest to practice toward husbands. A woman would not think of being unkind to a friend, because she treasures the friend's opinion of her. But a husband?

   Maxine came to me with tears of desperation, "I don't love my husband anymore. I just want out of this marriage. Everybody deserves some love in their life, don't they?" My reply was, "Yes, they surely do." I asked Maxine to agree to an experiment in loving. She was enthusiastic to try anything if it would make her life more tolerable.

   She asked, "How can I love him when I can't stand him around?" I told her God's Word says that being kind is loving. We mapped out a plan of action for his return home that evening. It called for Maxine to treat her husband as she would a good friend she was expecting. She would meet him with the attitude of friendliness, invite him into a house that was cleaned, and with children that were squared away, so they could have time together and coffee ready to serve.

   Three days later Maxine called me to say her whole life was changing before her eyes. Dinner was becoming an occasion to look forward to and she felt different toward Mike. She chose to be kind at home.

Has confidence in self—can trust others because of self-confidence.

Leave negative attitudes—jealousy, envy, haughtiness, arrogance, touchiness. A wife does not feel threatened if she is being the wife she wants to be. There is no need for comparison with other women. A wife working on the wife side of the court to her own satisfaction is like a magnet that draws her husband's thoughts and attention back to her. She has the advantage over other women in that she is bonded to her husband in marriage. And he has chosen to build a relationship with her.

Is content to be me—not always wishing to be like someone else.

If she spends her time wishing, she should try working from the vantage point of learning to like herself. Otherwise, she is wasting her time and also missing the opportunity of working out her own happiness.

Has a right evaluation of self—not conceited.

The standard for evaluation is from God's point of view, not checking out all of the failures around her for comparison. Remember God furnishes the fabric, pattern, and material with which she works. Hers is the cutting out, sewing, and fitting her life to *her.* This is a worthwhile project of cooperating with God.

Is generous—thoughtful of others' needs.

She must like who she is enough that she does not feel in the category of servant when her husband asks her to meet his needs.

Is always polite—uses good manners at all times.

Even with husband and children. A lot can be learned about her attitude of love by checking the manners she uses when only her husband is present. How is the listening? How is the speaking? How is the meal prepared and served?

Is not demanding of one's own way—considerate.

Consideration must begin with self. Resentments are stored when she does not give examination to how she feels. God does not take advantage of her. Demanding her own way usually comes when she lets others impose their ideas and standards on her without saying how she feels and what she thinks.

Is pleasant—enjoyable to be with.

Does he look forward to being with her because she is contributive and participating in building the relationship? This is brought about by being alert, fresh, listening, and attractive to him.

Is approachable—easy to communicate with.

Is open to hear what he chooses to share with her. The part of communication that is laborious is listening. A cartoon pictured two cave men with one saying, "Isn't it wonderful someone taught us to talk?" Next picture. The other replied, "Yes, but it is too bad someone did not teach us to listen." She must learn to be open to him. Listening to find out who he is, what he wants, and where he is going. Listening to understand him. Taking down her barriers to communication is hurtful but she is the only one that can take them down. Some of the barricades are: acting as if she knows what he is going to say and arguing with him about how he feels and what he thinks.

Is forgiving—settles differences immediately.

Takes her share of responsibility for and works from her side of the court to settle the disagreement. Not being afraid to ask forgiveness for wrong done to the relationship.

Will hardly notice others' wrong—not a fault finder.

Choosing to major on what he does that pleases her instead of harping on what displeases her. When this is actually spelled out, there is more right in the worst kind of relationship than we are usually ready to accept and deal with.

Is just—wants fairness above preferential treatment.

This takes the manipulating out of the relationship. This part of love causes her not to take unfair advantage because of what he may feel for her. In tennis it would be choosing not to "smash."

Is loyal—a friend at all times.

A friend is one who sees us as we are, and loves us still. If not a friend, then he must be classified as indifferent or an enemy.

Has confidence in one loved—believes the best.

This is working with the positives and not anticipating the negatives.

Expects the best of one loved—looks at what he does right.
When a mistake is made, we have a way of dwelling on it and
recalling it to mind many times. She usually takes it for granted
and expects her husband to do what is right without recalling or
commenting on the right. She needs to clearly indicate her confidence in him by taking time to express her appreciation for his
choice of what is right.

Always stands ground in defending one loved—not critical.
Criticism only works to destroy. Checking back over the characteristics of love, we find that with singularity it is giving in nature.

Love is a standard of living. We are concerned, or we should
be, about people who live on a sub-standard level. What about
the people who have a high standard of living with no joy of life?

Love is not automatic. We actually decide to love or not to love.
Love is a matter of will. Our desire to feel loved is made possible
when we decide to give love. When the will is set in motion, the
emotion of love is abundant.

Giving love is a *key* to happiness. While we look for the abundant
life in "things" or what others do for us, we are stumbling over
the truth that it is more blessed to give than to receive. You receive more happiness in giving than you do in getting.

A wife's responsibility is met when she has given her love to
her husband. What he does in return is *his* responsibility. There
is joy and happiness found in giving love. The return is doubled
when love is responded to.

Decide to love. Make it a matter of will. Love, unless it is given,
can never be felt. The promise of God is that the more love you
give, the more you will receive.

There are three kinds of love. The kind you get, the kind you
wish you had, and the kind you give. We must learn and re-learn,
decide and re-decide to *give* love. There is no end to the effort.
Hate needs no instruction but only waits to be provoked.

Husband's Needs

7
Husband's Needs

God's intention for woman to complete man is stated clearly in the Genesis account. I have read this explained away, rationalized, and contradicted. Yet, man is still seeking out a woman with which to share a lifetime completion.

If every man had the same needs, I am convinced God would have given "Ten Commandments to wives" on how to meet their husband's needs. Instead, He said for each wife to be submissive to her own husband. The husband is the one to spell out his need to her, and he is the only one who can do it accurately.

In the beginning of marriage, the needs he has are stated often. Sometimes he holds out for forty years, patiently or impatiently saying what his needs are. Some of the less hearty give up after a few years with, "What's the use—she doesn't listen." And they become the *quiet ones.*

Wives are shocked by what their husbands think and say. The first reactions when he feels differently from the way she does are to correct him, argue with him, or compete with him.

Since God did not make woman and man natural enemies, the struggle comes from rebellion at the idea of meeting his needs. To be defensive is not necessary. Hopefully, his intentions are not to hurt her, but to share what his needs are with her. She is free to do whatever she pleases in meeting those needs.

She must listen with her eyes, listen with her ears, listen with all of herself, because if she does not she is going to misunderstand what he is trying to communicate to her. The listening side of communication is almost a lost art. I feel one of the reasons is that it takes *total presence* to listen. This is the way her *whole person* gets involved with him.

Listening without response is not participating. She needs to respond as to how she is understanding and accepting what he is saying to her. The acceptance of her husband as the person he is gives her a basis for understanding what he is saying to her. One of our American freedoms is the right to our own opinion. None of us would want to give that up. We may choose to change that opinion, but we want the right to be heard. Let's be sure we have not denied our friend-husband his right in this area. He wants to express his opinions in a friendly atmosphere so he can sift them out and rearrange them to a better advantage for all concerned. Differing opinions can merge to the satisfaction of both when each party feels he is being heard and his opinions are worthwhile to the whole. Wives want just that kind of consideration. When she takes down her defenses (which comes about as she learns to like herself) she will become more accepting of him as a person.

Serious thought should be given to the responsibility a man assumes for leadership and guidance, which are his to maintain. Responsibilities when he says, "I do." He is saying, "This is the woman I want to share my entire life with. I will love her, provide for her, and lead in the marriage relationship."

We keep hearing that to assume the leadership and financial burden of the marriage is too great of a task for the man. Evidently most men do not think of it as any great hardship, but rather move out to meet the needs, without fanfare, as something they have planned to do.

Marriage is two individuals with their own personalities and ideas coming together, not to submerge one of them, but to bond together in a lifetime commitment of sharing. The self-preservation instinct is not necessary in this relationship. They have chosen to contribute to one another. What is advantageous to one is contributive to the other when they are working toward the union of the two.

The man needs a follower, not a fighter. He is not a perfect leader, nor is she expected to be a perfect follower. If she wants him to have a chance to become a good leader, she must give him a chance to practice by being a *supportive follower*.

Pardon my theology. When Eve picked the avocado in disobedience to God's command, she whipped up some guacomole, ran to the store, picked up some chips, and called Adam in from the garden for a snack. After he had eaten and realized what he had done, he tried to blame the whole scene on Eve, but God didn't let him get by with that. He made him responsible for himself. Because Adam listened to his wife and followed her into rebellion against God, He gave them both clear-cut definitions as to how they were to work together. God assigned the husband the place of providing and leading in the marriage relationship.

As women, we readily see the need of *one* president for each company. We realize that there must be organization in order for anything to be accomplished. We do not rebel at this in other areas of life, but cannot seem to accept the fact that God designated the husband as the head of this tie-in.

The alternatives that seem to be offered to us if we are not in control are in words like: subservient (acting in a subordinate capacity), submissive (passive "door mat"), or submerged (loss of identity to husband). With these words as a definition of her place as a follower, a wife begins to have the nagging feeling that she has the short end of the contract and is missing all of the good things in life.

In order for a husband to be able to *walk on* a wife, she must lie down and allow it. A door mat wife is saying, "I have no value in this relationship," or "I choose not to make any contribution to this marriage."

To set value of persons in order, we find that the first woman came from man, but every man since has come from woman. *Neither is to be rated second to the other.* However, organization is needed in order to move out to accomplish the relationship.

It would be a sad story if God had left woman to her own enlightenment, to work out her own dilemma by herself, but he did not. Even when she is disobedient, God still loves her and is concerned for her. God in all of his wisdom (which woman is still questioning) placed a head, protector, controller, director, manager, commander-in-chief, or whatever you choose to call him, over woman.

The Apostle Paul, in his letter to the Ephesians, pleads with woman to *submit* to her own husband. Today's woman yells back, "Submission—never!" If she could quit rebelling long enough to listen, she could hear Paul saying, "Wife, you have someone to refer to for his judgment or opinion, to turn to for aid, to call in, to ask for help, to talk things over with, to take up matters with, or to consult."

The Bible is also emphatic when it tells the older woman to instruct the younger woman how to be wise and how to *learn* to love her husband and children.

The Bible uses the word "submission" but not with a negative definition. When a woman comes to the place of choosing a husband, she is saying she has found someone she trusts and feels has her best interests at heart. And she wants to build her life with his.

To show a definition of "submit" outside of marriage, let's take a writer as an example. A writer works diligently over a manuscript to perfect it as far as she can. When she has completed it to her satisfaction, she submits it to an editor whom she trusts. The editor reads and marks the manuscript to be of help to her in communicating. The work is returned to the writer who must continue to work on her material if it ever is to be printed. The editor does not do the rewriting or call the writer stupid for asking help.

In marriage a wife has someone to turn to for help, for advice, for counsel, someone who is interested in helping her become a happy person. Why shouldn't she want to stick close to one who is interested in helping her to become all that she wants to be in the marriage.

Phyllis called to tell me she guessed they would be moving soon. She said, "I really don't want to go. It is not a good location, the housing is lousy, and it will be hard on the children to move, but Harry insists. How can he be so unreasonable?" All that judgment without many facts.

I asked if she had considered the shakiness of his position, the kind of work he was doing which he hated, his responsibility for providing for the family now and ten years from now, and the people with whom he worked. Her reply was, "No, I was thinking how inconvenient it was for the children and me." Inconvenience as compared to weightier matters such as food, clothing, shelter, education, security, retirement!

When a man steps back from a decision he knows he should make (for the sake of peace in the family or the happiness of his wife) and does not take the job or make the venture that he feels is for the good of all, he has paid a great price. He will begin to feel he has an enemy in his own marriage.

When he indicates a need and she does not consider that he should have the final say, then she is saying that he is not important to her. When I mention *final say,* I am not saying that she should not express herself. But I am saying that she should express herself in such a way that he is free to make the final decision as he feels it should be made.

Close relationships are not built without considering the other person. When he says that the job needs to be changed, he only proceeds with the details when he can be heard. Until a wife listens to all he is saying, she is not really prepared to give an intelligent response.

He will have taken the pieces apart to see if it is best. He will have considered everything that is wrong. He will likely have gone over every detail in his mind before he ever mentions it to her. He wants to know what she thinks and what she feels. He is not coming for a judgment of what he has expressed but new ideas from her point of view.

When she tells him what to do, she is communicating, "You are not capable of making a decision that will affect this family. I am capable, so I will make the decision."

Children follow the mother's example in the home. If she is rebellious to leadership, she cannot expect the children to be respectful of their father's decisions or of her decisions.

There are definite needs a husband has that only a wife can meet. This does not mean that she is responsible for all of his needs. As she listens to him and accepts him as he is, she is able

✓to contribute closeness, warmth, and love to the relationship. If a wife chooses to neglect his stated needs, she must be willing to let someone else meet those needs (and there are lonely women everywhere who would be glad to try), or he must go on with his needs unmet. Do you want to encourage your husband to have an affair?

Sharing self totally is a scary business for wife and for husband. It is for the wife because she is not convinced her husband has her best interests at heart. She is fearful of his ability to lead. She is not sure if she should follow and that he will not take advantage of her.

Husband's fears are somewhat different. The constant drain of *competing* instead of *completing* takes its toll on the desire to build a relationship. Man's judgment is not always best, but when a wife shares what she thinks and what she feels with him, he has a much better chance of leading in the right direction. Since God made the design, let not woman usurp man's authority as leader. A strategic position is that of following. As Joe expressed it one evening in a small group, "When Sue follows me another rung higher, I can't fall back. I am always aware of where she is and want to help her when she is having difficulty. I need her support."

✓Another fear deep within a husband is that his wife will not see him as a successful, worthwhile individual. He needs her reassurance of his standing with her.

The wife part of Ephesians 5:33 in *The Amplified Bible* reads, "And let the wife see that she respects and reverences her husband—that she notices him, regards him, honors him, prefers him, venerates and esteems him; and that she defers to him, praises him, and loves and admires him exceedingly."

He has a definite need for affirmation from her of what he means to her as her husband.

To have her displeasure with him as a person is a devastating blow. Any hint of her not liking him as a person causes him to withdraw from her and close himself off from her. His fear of being rejected by her is too great a risk for him. The relationship is hindered.

The following are a few areas that indicate rejection to a husband:

Arguing with him when he has already made a decision. Most women have had their husbands ask why they always argue with them—when the women felt they were only expressing how they felt and thought about what their husbands were saying. Did he ask for her opinion? Does she normally give others her opinion when it is not asked for? He will *not change* his decision by force after he has made it and feel good toward her. His only reason for changing it at all would be to keep *peace.*

The attitude that her business ability is keener than his in investing, buying, or selling.

Questioning the importance of father's role and the way he handles his role.

Acting as if he were a "dumb-dumb" if he has not read certain books, taken classes, or does not enjoy the same entertainment or music.

Disagreeing with him in the presence of others.

Parading his past failures as a leader.

Treating him with contempt as if he made no worthwhile contribution to the marriage—thus deserved no say in decisions.

Insulting him by talking about "going back to work," so she could have some of the "things" she wants, or because she is so unfulfilled.

Expressing no pleasure with his gift to her.

Not understanding when he wants more things for her.

Judging him an unbeliever because he does not act like she does.

His fears dissipate when:

She goes to him with what she feels and what she thinks as a contribution of information and not making a decision he can't afford to refuse.

She realizes that when she has fed information into his "computer" on how she feels and thinks that he is twice as equipped to make good business decisions.

"Completing" is giving information to him so he does not have a rival in his own camp.

She lets him be the father. God made fathers and He made

mothers. If both made the same contribution to the making of
a child or the raising of a child, one would not be necessary. A
child needs what a father gives. The wife needs to guard against
dictating what she thinks that role should be. It comes quite natural
for him when the husband/wife relationship is good. If he is too
hard on the child or too lenient, it may be his way of fighting
to preserve his own place as father.

She shares what she has learned that has been helpful to her,
not *what she feels he should hear for himself so he can change.*

She saves her disagreement until she is alone with him. The body
language kind and verbal kind, also.

*She compliments him on the things he does right and leaves him
to work out his own failings.* He is quite aware of his own short-
comings. Mentioning them again and again only irritates him.

*She spends time often remembering what he is contributing to
the relationship and comments to him about it.* (A busy mind can
choose to think on constructive things.)

*She is appreciative of what is already there and learns to enjoy
it.* Things without a good relationship will never bring happiness.

The gift without the giver is bare, because it is just an object.
We buy gifts as a means of expressing to another person that they
are special to us. Always receive the expression graciously. The
gift is secondary.

*She understands that accomplishing more, more, more meets a
need in him as a person.* He is also saying he thinks his wife deserves
the very best. Do not try to change or thwart this drive to excel.

*Women and men do not have the same physical growth patterns,
so do not expect them to have the same spiritual growth patterns.*
He does not have the same needs, so his actions will differ. (Don't
try to take God's place.)

Asking for forgiveness when wrong has been done is the way
to remove the barriers in a relationship. Only after forgiveness
has been asked can a healing and building of the relationship begin.

Battlegrounds: In-laws, Children, Finances, Sex

8
Battlegrounds: In-laws, Children, Finances, Sex

A battleground is where two enemies come together to fight out their differences. When warring in marriage, there is no winner—there is only a truce. That is, until a later day or more resentment is stored to be released, and the battle is on again.

Over what is the conflict? The threat is what marriage is all about from the beginning. Two people by their own choice have joined together to become *one* unit. When either side of that unit feels he or she is being moved into a secondary place, the battle begins. The competition for the place of leadership is also a part of the skirmish.

The three main causes of divorce are said to be in-laws, finances, and sex. Insurance against divorce is recognizing how these three areas of conflict can be dealt with as two people blend their lives together, instead of literally tearing each other apart.

IN-LAWS AND OTHERS

Special people in each of their lives can be the source of conflict. The instruction of the Bible is that husband/wife leave all others and come together as one. There are to be no ties that would rival this oneness for either husband or wife. The Bible does not labor the point four times about *leaving* parents and *cleaving* to mate just to have something to say. Rather, it emphasizes this necessity, for there must be harmony in the relationship.

Parents are a necessary part of life. They are God's way of creating and training children.

As the child matures into an adult and decides to establish his/her own home, the parents must do the cutting away at the request of the child, now an adult. This maturing process really starts at birth with the parent recognizing that the parent-child guidance relationship must be severed a little at a time. Failure to recognize this later causes heartache for both parent and child. A child tends to mature only as the parent lets go.

When a child remains a child in the eyes of a parent, even though he is grown physically, there is a strangling process going on.

What happens when parents put the child first in the relationship and do not build with each other as husband and wife? They will continue to pull on the child to provide their happiness, even though the child is grown and trying to build a marriage relationship of his own. This is obvious in the unhappiness when the children leave the home and in the high divorce rate in this problem category. Parents who build their lives around their children wreck two marriages.

One actual solution must come about as the child chooses to give first consideration to the marriage partner and acts this out, as well as verbalizes the decision. In a situation where her parents were constantly giving advice and calling for right responses from her, Lou came to me with, "Where do I begin? I know that Bill and I are always arguing about every decision we try to make, because he and my family are always in opposition to each other and I feel pulled apart." The action was not with Bill. The only person that could do anything was Lou. She could have made her stand with Bill verbally and acted on it each and every time there was a disagreement. Lou was the one who had not been given the freedom by her parents to build a marriage.

Children also cause conflict in a marriage if they are not in a secondary place. The right beginning is *husband first* before the child is born. Children are in the home on a temporary basis. They are there to be loved, trained, and enjoyed. A husband should never be put in the position of being competitive with his own child. Children are privileged indeed when parents recognize that they need to be taught independence from the beginning. Because children are in the home for a short period of time (18 to 20 years) it is a temptation to put them first. When this happens, the relationship of husband/wife suffers, the children are insecure, and the children are given a wrong pattern for their own marriage.

Women are taught to be good mothers and reminded by family and friends how they are to put the children first because they *need* them and cannot provide for themselves.

Terry, a young mother of three small children, asked me for ideas of how to deal with her mother, who was constantly wanting to have first consideration in her life. "I have my own family. I can't just run every time she calls. I am just torn apart all of the time because Mother tells me how unhappy she is because I am so far away from her."

Terry's mother has spent all of her time enjoying and doing for her children and failed to build even a casual relationship with her husband. Now that the children are gone out of the home, her life has no purpose unless they are having a part in it. Not only is Terry's mother miserable, she is making the new family have unnecessary conflict by trying to crowd into first place.

There are other relationships that clamor for first place, such as old friends, hobbies, careers, P.T.A., church organizations, civic clubs, and numerous other groups. Choose to end the competition and put husband in first place. When others question the need for this, it is not necessary to explain your reason, because the majority of them do not know what you are talking about and will only try to argue. It is your decision and you need explain it to no one or try to justify yourself.

Children and others will always be demanding your attention. Now is the time to begin teaching them that they have a special time. But so does their father and mother have a special time that is theirs alone. Let them know, not only by telling them but by example.

Pauline shared with me, "One evening I was in a big rush to get off to a meeting and I put paper plates on the table for the children and myself, but put a regular plate for my husband Jim." The children teased, "Big deal! Dad is the only one that rates." That same week Pauline said she heard the children remarking to their friends that their Dad really rated in their home. A year has gone by and occasionally one of them will refer to the evening of the special plate.

Plan to put your husband first. When a child is in control, he will always be the center of attention and very insecure. If a mother really loves her children, she will discipline (teach and train) them to see how valuable the husband/wife relationship is to her.

Disciplining the children is a major area of conflict. This is where it is necessary to see the value of two points of view—male and female. Observe how overprotective most mothers are. They want to keep their children on the sidewalk, even with a bicycle. They have the fear that something is going to happen to their children. They have a difficult time giving them their freedom.

A wife must trust her husband to help get the *little ones* out of the *nest*. It is part of his responsibility to help his children become independent.

Children are very crafty in playing one parent against the other. They usually ask what they want to do from the parent who is most likely to say "yes" that day. They need father and they need mother.

Discipline is an area where the parents need to decide on a course of action. Once decided, then the two must work together as a team. If she does not agree, it is absolutely necessary that she refrain from correcting his actions, verbally or via body language, in front of the child. Let the father be the father and the mother be the mother. Agree on what is going to be done and support one another. Consistency is a must in discipline. A wife should always feel free to share what she thinks about the discipline, but she does not have the right to take charge of the whole program herself. The father has the God-given responsibility for the leadership of the home.

The security level of the child is hindered when parents do not work together in disciplining. The child gets a pattern and a guideline for his life from seeing the parents as they work together.

It is not necessary for a wife to always agree with her husband in order for them to have a good marriage. The last thing that she should do is to let someone else know when she is disagreeing with him, instead of sharing it with him. He is the one that she disagrees with and he is the one that should be told. She needs to tell him when she does not feel he is doing right, or that it hurts her, or that she does not agree with what he is saying. But she must let him know that she is going to work with him as a person, because they are building a relationship, and the only way she can help is by doing her part. She must not be judgmental every time he makes a decision. She does not experientially know one thing about being a father, even if she has read all of the books about fatherhood, because she is not a man. She will best spend her time letting father be father. She will add the mother's touch, because that is where her skills are.

Once discipline has been decided on, it must be followed. The child learns how to follow by the mother's attitude. One of the reasons children are undisciplined is they are following the easy "line of least resistance." Remember in the game of follow-the-leader, the entire game is fouled up when there are two leaders. When mother decides to set up a second set of rules to be used when the father is out of the home, the child becomes totally confused. When the mother sets up her own rules, it doesn't take the child long to decide that he does not want to be a follower. This causes chaos in the home and emotional problems in the child.

No greater gift can be given to children than to have a mother and father standing together and loving each other.

Anytime another person is given first consideration over the husband, it automatically causes the other person to become his rival. The husband often begins the battle to win first place so that he and his wife can again work constructively on the relationship.

One part that a wife can fulfill is putting her husband first in her life. The struggle is over when he has been given what he is seeking, and both are winners.

FINANCES

"If he can waste money on boats, then I have a right to spend foolishly, too," Martha blustered. Finance is a battleground on which much of our resentment can be aired with the feeling it is justified.

Money is not really that big of a problem—but who is in charge and how important they are to each other as husband and wife is of utmost importance. Whether a yearly income of $1,000,000 or $10,000, there is conflict unless the two are working together.

Whose money is it that we are battling over? If we are working to become one unit with two sides then it belongs to both. It is *our* money. If we are trying to maintain separateness and become one, we are defeated already because there is *no* trust. The unit working together establishes guidelines and responsibilities and then both parties understand where their working area is.

In his mind, man has usually settled what he feels his financial responsibilities are before he asks her to marry him. He plans to be the main provider and the manager of the money. This is often discussed before marriage in a counseling session, but effort is not usually made to draw up any type of plan on their own.

Control of the money is his way of saying, "I am going to be the leader. If I make the money, I am going to say how it will be spent." He is also trying to say in a last-ditch stand, "I am important to your welfare, whether you recognize it or not."

The majority of wives begin to control the finances in the first year of marriage. This is brought about as he is made to feel inferior because of her criticism. Even though she may have better judgment in finances than he does, I am made to wonder: is this not the standard of what is important to her instead of what is best for the marriage relationship?

If a wife is in control of the finances, she is in the leader position. This means she is off of her side of the court. Some questions she needs to consider are: 1) What attitude does she have toward her husband? 2) Is he really inadequate in her eyes as a manager? 3) Is he successful to her?

"When Mabel says she must manage the finances, she is the same as yelling from the housetop that I am incapable of handling the finances, and that is hard to take," Al remarked to the counselor.

"I am providing well. It is that she is just never satisfied—she always wants more."

The conflict gets all out of proportion when the husband is providing the money, and the wife is asked to manage if she has no means of increasing the amount needed. This could be called a "pressure hold" or a tactic in the battle to put her in an untenable position.

It was this kind of a situation that caused Jerry to scream, "New tires again? It has only been three years. We just don't have that kind of money to spend."

A wife managing all of the finances has a burden on her that is unfair. Bookkeeping is another thing if we identify that as writing checks to pay the monthly bills.

Budgeting is a necessity if we are to stay off of the battlefield. This allows a plan of work. This way the *how much, for what* is decided by both, and there is a working together with a leader leading and a follower participating.

Whether or not the wife works should be a decision that is made together, since both are affected. This needs to be reconsidered if children are brought into the home. They deserve emotional security as well as financial security, and this is not possible with the mother giving her best outside of the home. Love cannot be dispensed to a child like a weekly allowance.

A wife should be responsible for a part of the money in order to sense her sharing. The idea that she is not a valuable part because she does not have a pay check is destructive. Worth does not always have a dollar sign. I feel the minimum amount of responsibility should be grocery money. It is a worthwhile challenge to stay within a grocery budget and have attractive, appetizing, well-balanced meals.

When a wife works, it is absolutely necessary that the "our money" concept be emphasized. Women like the "our money" idea until they receive *their* check and it is very easy to switch to "my money because I have earned it."

For both husband and wife there should always be a specified amount that is to be spent with complete freedom without giving account to each other.

SEX A BATTLEGROUND?

Yes, because it is the only time and place some husbands feel first with their wives. Some husbands are accused of being, and may seem to be, over-sexed because they are demanding to know they are number one. Knowing a husband's need, some wives use sex as a weapon to gain their own selfish way.

Sexual needs can only be met in marriage, and still maintain a high opinion of one's self and be fulfilling. In 1 Corinthians 7, Paul teaches that the bodies of husband and wife belong to each other. We actually give away the sexual rights to do as we please without thought of the other when we marry. The Bible is very explicit in declaring that nothing is to take the place of meeting the sexual needs of each other in marriage. The Apostle Paul goes so far as to say that not even praying or fasting is to interfere in the relationship—except it be by agreement, and then only for a limited time.

One of the reasons sexual promiscuity is so damaging is the giving away of something that belongs to another.

A wife may know all about her physical side and have read technique books galore, and not be informed at all about the emotional needs to be met within herself and her husband in the sexual relationship.

A bride needs to give consideration to the fact that she may have protected herself all of her young woman years and it will take some time to adjust to belonging and giving to her new husband. The basic need to be loved and cherished is one that causes a woman to want to become a wife. She has a desire to be that very special person, to be told that she is the one and only woman for him.

She should understand that the enjoyment of intercourse is a shared responsibility. She must become involved with more than his feeling of enjoyment. She must call all of her faculties together and concentrate on her own enjoyment. We average around 150 words a minute in speaking. During intercourse, if a wife is mentally sewing, cooking, cleaning, planning the next day's activities, or whatever her immediate project is, she cannot expect to fully enjoy sex.

What a husband is saying to his wife when seeking intercourse needs some interpretation. Her "Oh, not again" attitude must be thought through. She should recognize that she is special because he has chosen to express his oneness with her. There are women literally on every corner, in every office, or wherever he may be that are beckoning to him, but he chose to come home. Sexual intercourse is one act that only the two of you share. No one else is included. This is a first place union achieved with each other. There are many books being written today on how to turn a husband on sexually. The problem in many homes is not how to turn him on but what to do with him when he is turned on?

Men are stimulated by sight, the clothes a woman wears that are attractive to him, her manners, the warmth of her personality, the smell of her perfume. She uses all of these means of turning his attention her way before marriage, but sometimes forgets how important it is to continue to turn his head her way after marriage.

"Oh, that's why Joe asks me, 'Why do you always look and smell so good when you are going out to a P.T.A. meeting when it is mostly women?' I thought he was complaining about the expense of the perfume or my being gone so much," Evelyn said. "Now that I think back, I go to bed in curlers, raggedy p.j.'s, and never waste my expensive perfume at home." To a husband this screams out that even the casual acquaintance or a complete stranger is more important to her than he is.

It would be helpful for her to remember that her desire for him is a big drawing card. He likes and wants to be wanted and needed sexually by her. Of all the areas in his life in which he wants to succeed with her, it is in feeling that he is capable of fulfilling all of her sexual desires. Because of his desire for success in this area, any criticism of his drive or lack of aggressiveness hinders his expression of himself. A husband who reads his wife to be saying he is a failure as a lover will cease to be her lover for fear of failing.

Some of the ways she turns him off she does not even realize. The constant checking to see if his response to her is genuine. Saying, "Make love to me, but let's don't have sex." Complaining about health, children, tiredness, *busyness,* his lacking in any area. Being passive toward him with, "Anything you want to do is okay by me."

Rare is the woman who has just the right amount of sexual activity. It is usually too much or too little. The frequency of the sex act needs important consideration. A wife is to meet all his sex needs. If he requested food because he was hungry, would she deny it to him because she had no appetite?

Intercourse meets an emotional need as well as a physical need. The emotional is sometimes the more important because it affirms more clearly that he is in first place with her and that she is willing to work toward a completeness with him. There will be problems that must be overcome in order to have intercourse that is satisfying to both.

Come out of "dullsville" and be creative. Here are two unique individuals in marriage and each should come up with their own contributions as to what is good for the two. What expresses their love and desire best? A wife should do her own survey to find what appeals to her husband in the way of clothes and actions.

While she is surveying, she would do well to remember that the most romantic thing she can do for her husband is *give him her total presence. Be there.* When she is all there, participating, there will soon be little to be desired. It takes two to have a good experience and only one to ruin it.

The beauty of 1 Corinthians 7:3-5 can be ruined if it is interpreted to mean you have a duty that must be performed. Duty sex is almost worse than no sex at all. First, it is a bum deal for the wife. It causes the *it's a man's game attitude.* Mothers who have failed to have a good sex experience pass this idea along to their children by subtle comments and negative actions. It is not a giving, loving experience for either, but a taking because she feels she *has* to give.

Background differences must be taken into consideration. The patterns that both of their parents have made for them must be considered. It is not to be a repeat of two sets of parents, but a whole new relationship for the two of them. The background of each takes time to unravel and reweave into what each of them desires for their own oneness.

There is a 5:30 p.m. depression that comes over many wives. They blame small children, a busy day of activities, strenuous work, you name it for their extreme fatigue. The main problem is not the amount of work but the fact that she hates to see her husband coming home because of the demands he will make on her. Would she be as tired if a friend knocked at her door and asked her to do something for her? Probably not.

She is worn out carrying all of her stored up resentments toward her husband because of past sexual activities that have not been meaningful to her. If tiredness were the real problem, a few minutes of relaxation could be arranged prior to her husband's return home, and all would be well.

Bad times in the bedroom also are built up when she has the fantasy that "he gets to go out into the big, wonderful world while I have to be tied to drudgery at home."

Pre-marital sex, especially when pregnancy resulted, is a problem that must be faced in building a good sex adjustment in marriage. In order to guide children to prevent this from happening, many parents teach them sex is wrong—instead of stating the facts as they are that sex before marriage is wrong. It is wrong because it hinders the adjustment in marriage plus many other reasons. To help you teach your children in this area, I recommend two excellent books, *Sexual Understanding Before Marriage* by Herbert J. Miles (Zondervan) and *Evelyn Duvall's Handbook for Parents* (Broadman).

A young woman at times agrees to pre-marital sex because the young man tells her how very much he loves her. After marriage she is haunted with the questions, "Why did he marry me? Did he really love me? Have I trapped him? Have I taken advantage of him or him of me?" All of the guilt and condemnation of self

begins to erode the relationship. Guilt can ruin what would otherwise be a good marriage.

God has made special provisions for dealing with guilt so that
an individual who has failed does not have to become a failure.
Jesus came in order that we might have access to God. Through
him the believer can acknowledge her sin (breaking of God's law)
and desire to be restored to fellowship with him by confessing
to God. According to 1 John 1:9, when she confesses God is faithful
and just to forgive and to cleanse her. She is as if she had never
sinned in God's sight. God says that He will not remember the
sin again. When a believer continues to be guilt-ridden, she is saying
that God is not able or will not forgive her. She needs to accept
God's forgiveness and spend all of her thought processes building
a good relationship, instead of rehashing something that God has
remedied.

God wants every woman to be a happy wife. He loves us. *Now*
is what she has to work with. Does her husband love her today?
She needs to love him and find out instead of trying to convince
herself that he does not.

Statistics reveal that there is not even a day's difference in the
frequency of need for sex between women and men. Too seldom
or too often to her liking indicates there is a deeper problem than
scheduling. She is not considering the needs of her husband in
relation to her needs, but is judging him by her standard of need.

Three great fears a woman has with regard to sex are: being
"used," being taken for granted, and unwanted pregnancy. The fear
of being used comes from statements she has heard from unhappy
women who feel that sex is a necessary evil. She needs to realize
that if sex is all her husband wanted, he could have his desire
satisfied many times over by other women. Sex is not enough.
He has a desire to build a lasting, close relationship with the woman
he has chosen to be his wife. I have found in seminar groups that
men do not have the fear of being "used" sexually. They are so
happy for their wives to desire them that all they can think of
is expressing themselves in return.

She fears that if she meets all his needs, he will expect a good sex expression regardless of how he may treat her.

Tom comes home and says to Nancy, "I am hungry. Is there anything ready to eat?" Nancy responds by preparing something that she knows he likes to eat. Tom comes home and says to Nancy first by his actions and then by words, "Let's make love!" Nancy retorts, "Forget you, you don't need to make love!"

The fellow that is "grabbing" all of the time is saying, "I have to grab while I can because she will never be willing." Denice handled the situation this way by saying, "The better meal you provide the more he enjoys eating. The more he enjoys eating, the more I want to cook." That principle applies to your sex life, too.

With all that is known about birth control there still must be a sharing of this responsibility since it does make a difference to the wife. Children should be wanted by both and the marriage should be on a steady basis for all concerned.

I am thankful that life is not all needs and problems, and that there are solutions and answers from the wife's side of the bed. Where she is on the road is not as important as being headed in the right direction.

Being of sound mind she can learn. She can learn to enjoy sex by making a mental note of what is pleasing to her and what is pleasing to her husband. She can learn when experiences are displeasing to find out why. When she fails, she must look for the reason. She can learn what to give up and what to add. She can make her own enjoyment a special project. Her husband will be willing to share in that project because more enjoyment for her means more enjoyment for him.

She can change and break the old patterns if she wants to change. It is also possible to change from a night person to a day person. "I am glad to have you home early, *but* don't ask me to get out of my routine because it just upsets my whole day," was Carolyn's greeting to Mike when he came home early just to be with her. He was so upset with her that he went out to play golf, was late getting home, and paid her no attention the remainder of the evening. She said to me, "I can't just drop everything and lock the bedroom door. What will the neighbors think?" I asked, "What difference does it make what the neighbors think? Are you more interested in them or a spontaneous relationship with your husband?" She can change. She cannot change husband, circumstances, or past, but she can change her own attitude toward sex.

A big reason that many women do not enjoy sex is they do not *think* about what they are doing. Jane asked in a class discussion, "Why is it a man doesn't let a headache bother his sex relationship?" Stop and think about it for a while. Unless he is totally involved in what he is doing, he has nothing to offer, so he keeps his mind on what he is doing.

Unless she chooses to become a totally involved woman, she really doesn't have anything to offer, either. She barely gets by and doesn't even realize how much she is missing. A woman is passive in the relationship when she lets her mind wander through the day's activities, goes over the children's problems, or what she plans to do tomorrow, instead of *concentrating* on enjoying what she is doing. She thinks she can get by and her husband will never know. Many times he is trying to help her achieve orgasm when she is not even interested enough to keep her mind on what she should be trying to accomplish.

Concentrate on what? On enjoyment for herself. She owes it to the marriage to learn about the construction of her own body.

In Sexual Understanding Before Marriage, Dr. Miles plainly discusses the fact that God created women with reproductive organs and sexual organs, which have specific functions. Dr. Miles gives eight sets of biological evidence that I would encourage you to read.

"In order to see this evidence, let us distinguish between (1) the female reproductive organs and their functions and (2) the female sexual organs and their functions. Let us note the major differences. When we examine the facts involved, it is clear that in the purpose and plan of the Creator, the female reproductive system and the female sexual system were to be two separate systems with two separate functions. This idea is similar to biologists' talking in terms of the respiratory system and the digestive system. Although these two systems are definitely related, they may be thought of as two separate systems with two separate functions . . . In the past we have thought of the female reproductive and sexual natures as operating together in one completely integrated unit. As a result of this false thinking, the female reproductive system has been greatly abused. Many unwanted children have been brought into existence. Likewise, the female sexual system has been greatly abused in that female sexuality was limited to the point that women did not enjoy the sexual system as God intended when He created woman." [1]

It is time that we come away from the misteaching that has been done in the name of Scripture to see that reproduction is not the only reason for sex. God made man and woman for each other and to enjoy each other and build a relationship with each other that is to last a lifetime.

A wife needs to be thankful for the opportunity of the relationship with her husband. She can set some goals 1) to overcome her hang-ups one at a time, 2) to be thankful for a husband who cares enough to want her to find her own enjoyment, 3) to ask for his suggestions and try them, 4) to ask him if he will help her with what interests her, 5) to major on concentrating to seek enjoyment for herself.

If I could use only one word to help a woman have a better sex experience, it would be *concentrate.* Concentrate on the man. Concentrate on her own enjoyment. Concentrate on the love that is between them. Concentrate.

A trap a woman may fall into is the attitude, "It does not matter whether I enjoy sex or not as long as he enjoys himself." That is not really being honest with herself. Before she knows it, she will have a nice supply of resentment stored away from this kind of rationalization. This is where she gets that "being used" feeling. It does matter. A wife must become involved on an enjoyment level for herself.

Variety is salvation from boredom. I love hamburger meat, but if I had to eat it the same way everytime it was served, it wouldn't take long for me to lose my appetite. One's husband is a resource person for ideas. Dr. Miles also has a technique book on sex from a biblical view, *Sexual Happiness in Marriage.* Dr. John W. Drakeford has written a valuable resource, *Made for Each Other,* which interprets sexuality in terms of biblical concepts.

A helpful way to determine where the real source of the problem is between a wife and her husband is to inventory the areas of conflict and see if he is really *Number One* in her life. When a wife is unwilling to put her husband in first place in her life, she is acknowledging that the relationship between them is not as important to her as it needs to be to build a good marriage.

If he is #1 with her, then there is a desire to work through the difficulty between them to a satisfactory solution.

---

¹Herbert J. Miles, *Sexual Understanding Before Marriage* (Grand Rapids: Zondervan Publishing House, 1971). Used by permission.

Description of a Happy Wife

9
Description of a Happy Wife

Mirror, mirror, on the wall, how is a happy wife supposed to look?

The common concept of a wife is taken from the cartoon section of life. She is tired looking, her hair is in curlers or stringing down. She is in some kind of sloppy outfit, angry, yelling at the kids, griping at her husband or shoving him out the door or complaining about him to her friend.

The picture is always negative. Why? Because people laugh. Why do they laugh? Because, for a great part of the time, this is the way the wife sees herself—so she identifies with the cartoon. She reasons, "It is better to laugh than to cry." She is not happy with herself. When she is not happy with herself, she does look less than her better self.

The description of a happy wife is singularly important to her because it is her life. She must know what she wants before she can begin to work toward her goal. She is the one who is responsible for whether or not she attains her goals.

Women think they know what their husbands want by listening to comic take offs on what *every* man expects his wife to be:

Always beautiful and cheerful. Could have married a movie star but wanted only him. Hair that never needs curlers or beauty shops. Beauty that won't run in a rainstorm. Never sick. Just allergic to jewelry and fur coats. Insists that moving the furniture by herself is good for her figure. Expert in cooking, cleaning house, fixing the car or TV, painting the house, and keeping quiet. Favorite hobbies, mowing the lawn and shoveling snow. Hates charge plates. Her favorite expression:

"What can I do for you, dear?" Thinks he has Einstein's brain
but looks like Mr. America. Wishes he would go play golf
with the boys so she could get some sewing done. Loves him
because he is so-o-o sexy.

Most men laughingly agree and go along with the joke. But
privately they say that they want a happy wife, above all else.

A very depressed friend of mine had a little girl move over close
to her and say, "Why did you make yourself that way?" My friend
realized that even a small child can tell how unhappy you are
by your face, how you dress, your posture, and your attitude. A
smiling face does not necessarily mean she is happy *if* she only
wears her *happy face* when she is outside the home. A scolding
face says something is wrong inside. Everyone in direct contact
with her had better watch their step because she is not pleasant.
This conveys to a husband, upon entering the door, that there
is unpleasantness to be dealt with, or he may choose to ignore
her and spend his time with the television all evening.

How a woman dresses also indicates how she feels about herself.
Sloppy clothes that have seen their better day, hair disheveled,
no makeup (in order to do her work) says she classifies herself
as a nobody kind of servant. Even first class domestics wear a
uniform.

Always lounging in a robe mirrors that she does not consider
herself to be important. She is usually overdramatizing by making
a production out of the fact that her job is unimportant in comparison to others. Looking like a scrub woman in order to clean the
floor tells how she feels about the definition of her job description.

The image she paints of herself causes her husband to feel she
is sharing sufficiently or insufficiently with him. How she feels
about her responsibilities and how she dresses to carry out her
tasks also affect her children.

Because I have two very lovely daughters, my friend Mildred
asked me for help with the way her eight-year-old daughter wanted
to dress for school. She said, "All she ever wants to wear is the
grubbiest jeans and a tee shirt. She says that is what all of the

other girls wear. What can I do?" I asked Mildred what she has on at home when Nancy leaves for school. Her reply, "Grubby jeans and a tee shirt." Mildred decided to wear a dress, fix her hair, and make up before breakfast, and found Nancy requesting new dresses and skirts to replace the jeans in a short period of time.

Daughters may pick up the style lines, but they mainly take a code of dress from their mothers. Sons also determine what is feminine as they see their mother's example.

A woman cannot alleviate all of the pressure of the children's peer group, but she can set standards from which her children can choose. The patterns may be ignored now but will be given due consideration as the children grow into maturity.

I am not suggesting that a woman go around in her best dress or suit, but I am saying she should be coordinated—matching—all together, because she feels better about her position if she looks nice to herself.

Attitudes are contagious. As communicable as measles. How a wife feels about herself sets the mood of the home, her attitude toward her husband, and whether or not happiness resides there. When she decides not to be in control of herself and just let "come what may" it will end being a negative, unhappy situation the majority of the time.

She decides to view her husband, as he enters the house, as a man tired from the day's activities or an old meany coming home just to pick on her. If she chooses the latter, it means her resentment is taking control.

A wife without knowingly doing it stores up resentment toward her husband when she expects him to make her happy. Resentment is a dangerous disease and can be fatal to the marriage.

"I don't know what is hindering our relationship—really I don't," and Marge was serious. "What stands between you that you wish he would take care of so you could be happy?" I asked Marge. There is no way that an outsider could answer that question for her. It is merely the matter of her getting the resentment out so she will quit reacting to things that are not important.

Freedom to be happy comes when we are willing to ask forgiveness for our part of the hurt, or for dwelling on it a long time, or for being unforgiving toward him. Also, asking her husband what his definition of a happy wife is will give her much needed information. It requires self-discipline for her to listen to him, because many times he may express the opposite direction to which she is committed.

His input is invaluable to her because she is his wife. In order to build a life together, it is necessary that both agree on the materials to be used. Both husband and wife are contributing to the relationship.

Most every husband has a primary concern about the happiness of his wife. The sharing of her desire to work out her own happiness will free him to be more expressive of his love for her.

If she should read all of the books that have been written about marriage, she would still have a blank space that can only be filled in by her husband. He has needs that are unique to him, needs that only he can tell her.

In October, 1974, the newspapers ran headline stories on the fact that Canadian Prime Minister Trudeau's wife felt trapped in her role. Wearing on her nerves was the lack of fulfillment in endeavoring to anticipate all of the expectations others had for her life.

This beautiful young "first lady" with ten people in her household staff, security guards, a husband with the top position in his country was trapped just like many other women who have far less with which to work. She was trapped trying to please everyone around her, and yet failing to identify herself and what was right for her as the wife of one man, Pierre Elliott Trudeau.

Is wife a good category to be in? To me it all depends on how you see yourself. If you are looking at what you have to offer, someone who loves you to work with, and the opportunities of planning and carrying out your goals together, it is the best place in the world to be.

In the metropolitan area of Orange County, California, I do

not dare drive to a speaking engagement without first consulting a map for specific streets to follow. A general idea will never get me there. I have wasted time and put extra strain on my heart from rising blood pressure trying to get off a freeway at the right point. There have even been times when I decided I could not get *there* from *here*. Such has not been the case when I made my plan of travel before I left my house.

Since it is a marriage of both, it is needful for both to share in what is desirable to each. One prominent excuse for not setting goals is that one cannot expect to be happy all of the time. Or we do not want to be hemmed in—we are flexible people. It is not a wife's responsibility to set marriage goals for the two of them but only for herself, unless she is sharing jointly with her husband.

A wife should have short-term goals like learning to plan menus a week at a time, or getting areas cleaned, or accomplishing a reading or sewing project, or becoming involved in an area that interests her. It is good for her to set down long-term goals like losing X number of pounds by a stated date or an endeavoring to develop a talent she feels she has.

Her goals when planned alone should be things that affect only her side of the marriage relationship. Volunteering her husband's services sometimes proves an embarrassment and adds hurt to the relationship.

No goals—no progress. Good marriages *do not just happen.* They must be planned and the plans must be worked. This prevents the often-heard comment, "I just can't understand where our marriage went wrong!"

A wife needs initiative to solve her own problems. To run outside the relationship of husband/wife for an answer from another person may be saying the husband is the problem. If this is what she thinks, then she is transferring her needs to someone else to meet them for her. She should set out in her present circumstance with determination to find an answer within the framework of her marriage, seeking the help of her husband.

A happy wife is one who has learned to see her own worth

and likes herself in the place she has chosen. She is working toward realizable goals which she has set for herself. She feels the love of her husband, because she is giving of herself to the relationship. These are the valuables of life.

Household Manager—Enjoyable Place to Be

10
Household Manager—Enjoyable Place to Be

Any job or position a person chooses should have enjoyment as well as fulfillment. I want to give you a few ideas as a starter on how to enjoy being a wife, work and all.

Available time is a term with which we are all familiar. It shows how much time we have to complete a job. Time is the one thing that is equally allocated to one and all. Whether rich or poor, tall or short, black or white, we all have twenty-four hours a day without exception. What we do with our time is the problem. We have two choices. We can invest our time or waste our time. The decision is made according to what is valuable to you and what goals you have set for yourself.

Planning is necessary in order to put time to the best use. Today is what we have to work with. As a young wife who was self-disciplined, I planned my schedule to include school, housework, and marriage. The only problem with my planning was the professors, friends, husband, and even strangers did not work with my schedule. As I was unable to complete my plans for Monday, I moved them over and added them to Tuesday's list. By Saturday I was totally swamped, plus being frustrated and overworked. I had not figured out that there needs to be flexibility in schedules. I also learned you can plan too much and feel defeated, regardless of how much you may have accomplished.

To be a good household manager, a woman must be in charge of her own time. She is bombarded constantly with demands for her time and attention.

People—husband, children, parents, friends, or neighbors—cannot take her time unless she allows them to do so. She must stay in control of her own time. Attitude is crucial if there is to be control of and enjoyment in work that must be done.

A wife without priorities is like a bride without a recipe. She fails the biggest part of the time. Any successful company has set priorities in order to reach the production goals. Any household, in order to be liveable, must be guided by priorities.

As a guideline in setting priorities use three catagories: 1) Have to, 2) Need to, 3) Want to.

The *have to's* must take first place on the list. The dishes must be washed. Even if in a dishwasher, they still do not jump in by themselves (Sometimes I wish they did.) The bed must be made. (It takes two or three minutes when you first get up.) Meals must be prepared. The house must be cleaned or straightened. Today may be the day for laundry. All items on the list of *have to's* should be things that must be done today without fail.

If there are small children in the home, be careful not to get an imbalance of things over persons, or vice-versa.

Suppose it is the middle of the morning and a friend calls with an invitation to lunch and your *have to* list is lagging. What to do? You rationalize that you need a break or maybe your friend needs someone to talk to.

Many women see no need for schedules because no one is checking to see if they are doing a good job. In fact, when a woman is feeling low she may say, "No one ever notices if the house is clean anyway, so what does it matter?" Or she may say, "My husband doesn't care about how the house looks." When a woman operates her household on a *feeling-like-doing-it basis,* it denotes she is very unhappy with the entire responsibility.

There are few wives who would not be upset with their husbands if they decided to go to work or not to go to work on a *feeling-like-it basis.* Society labels him a bum or lazy. What he would be is irresponsible.

A woman does not really feel a sense of worthwhileness in her life if she is not working toward and accomplishing some goals. *Have to's* are a part of every life.

If you are a wife with a career check yourself often. Be sure all of your sense of accomplishment is not outside your relationship with your husband. There are *have to* requirements that are necessary for every woman to be satisfied with herself in the role of wife.

The *need to's* list is made up of things that must be done occasionally, not every day. Such things as washing windows, mending, organizing shelves, drawers, or closets. One should be scheduled each day, so you will not be overcome with hopelessness by trying to do them all the same day. This kind of organization calls for cleaning one drawer at a time. Or washing the windows in one room at a time. Before I learned how to schedule the *need to's*, I took two or three days to clean my kitchen from ceiling to floor, shelf paper, waxing—the whole thing. I had a fabulously clean kitchen for a few days as opposed to the present *need to* time which keeps my kitchen neat at all times.

It is amazing what can be accomplished in the few minutes you have to wait while others fit into your schedule. Using your time constructively beats building resentments that consume extra time. The Agricultural Extension Service, a branch of the State University, in your community has many short-cut ideas and helpful hints which are free to you.

Enlist children in the home as a matter of training for them and also as a help to you. They can do assigned tasks when they have been properly instructed about what an acceptable job is. Please do not leave them on their own until they have been shown the procedure for doing the work.

"I never get to do anything I *want to do*," says that woman who is not organized. A career wife spends about three-and-one-half hours doing the same tasks a wife in the home all day takes twelve hours to accomplish. One is organized while the other is helter-skelter. There should be room for one *want to* in every day. Occasionally there will be *want to* time for an entire day.

Household tasks should not take the place of working on the marriage relationship. A clean, well-organized household is no substitute for a warm, growing rapport. Values must be straight in order to set priorities that grow a better working together of husband and wife.

A woman's work is never done unless she plans and works.

Work falls into three categories: drudgery, necessary and creative.

Drudgery is something that must be done, but is undesirable. This job should be done first because dreading to do a chore drains more energy than the actual work of the job. To begin with, the least desirable undertaking removes some of the pressure from that day.

Necessary next. These are those tasks that *have to* be done, but are classified as neither a good experience nor a bad experience.

Creative part last because that is the area where you receive the most reward for yourself. You can spend the extra time here and enjoy it more because there is nothing hanging over your head.

To begin scheduling yourself, I would recommend a written routine. After it begins to be a habit, you can carry it on quite well mentally, but at first you need to see it written out. A day by day of *have to's, need to's,* and *a want to.*

Begin light. You need a flexible schedule of what you hope to accomplish each day at first. As a young wife, I made my schedule as if I had two other people helping me (which I did not). One evening I fell into bed with exhaustion and complained, "I have not accomplished a thing today." My husband's sympathetic words were, "What happened?" For the next five minutes I related my busy day. His comment was, "It sounds like to me that you have had a very busy day and been very effective." Realizing what I had carried through that day, I said to him, "What I really mean is that I did not complete everything that I had planned to do today." This kind of an experience is what causes women to give up and quit trying to get organized. I call it the "harried housewife syndrome"—hopeless, so why try?

Don't you dare sit down with that best-seller first or you will be hating yourself about the time for everyone to return home. Stick with each job until it is completed, and then you will really enjoy the book.

"No, Nancy, I can't talk with you now, I will call you later." (That means when you have finished the dishes. Nancy may think you have gone out of your mind, but is is *your time* and you make your own priorities.)

Limit telephone calls to your schedule. There is nothing rude about telling a friend you are free to talk for ten minutes. You are giving her an opportunity to share anything that is important. At the same time, you are saying your time is important. You do not owe other people an explanation of your priorities. Very little is ever accomplished without *schedule and work,* be it washing dinner dishes or an extravaganza of some sort.

Hard work never killed anyone but sometimes you feel that you will be the first victim. Take heart. Work is healthy for body and mind. The required work of the day can be accomplished, when priorities are set and followed through on, in the matter of three or four hours. Freedom is then yours to use the time left with a free conscience and a sense of accomplishment.

Preparation of meals is taxing on the energies. One of the reasons it is such a strain is because of the dread of doing it daily. Four o'clock in the afternoon is the low place of the day for the woman who does not know what she is going to have for dinner that evening. For a really great lift, try planning seven main meals with lunch and breakfast thrown in. Plan snacks if children are there. With a calendar in hand and the coming week's activities listed, this can be the most valuable hour of the week's pursuits as you decide on the food consumption of your family. This is a special boost to the wife who is busy with her own interests outside the home.She makes her meal planning, preparation, and eating a good experience for herself and her family without spending extra emotional energies that end up making her irritable.

Posting the snack of the day will give the children guidance, as well as something to look forward to after school. It will keep them from emptying the shelves in one afternoon. If the budget is limited, (whose isn't), set only one day a week for sharing treats with their friends.

Menus for the week posted on the bulletin board or refrigerator door enlist every member of the family. When you decide to change, be sure you change the posted menu. Keep it flexible. Let them make suggestions for the coming week.

Some of my students have made fun time of meal planning with all the family sharing ideas written down in the form of a list to draw from for future use. This becomes the master list from which one can plan. One needs to keep a running list of the number of ways to prepare hamburger, chicken, ham, meatless casseroles, etc. Each time you remember something you have not prepared in a long time, you can add it to your list until the meal planning becomes enjoyable instead of a last-minute, brain-racking experience.

When the planning of what to serve is finished, a shopping list should be made. Pull the recipes from your file and check the needed ingredients so you are sure when the day arrives for spaghetti that you have everything on hand to make the sauce. Nothing is more frustrating than to start a meal and have to run to the market or next door, or substitute because you have not planned well.

Once-a-week shopping will save you money—more than that, it will take a load off of you, a load you probably do not even realize you are carrying.

Lack of planning causes a wife to work under extra tension. Until she decides what is to be served for dinner that evening, she is under added stress. An everyday trip to the grocery store makes food cost at least one-fourth more and gives that thrown-together look on the table. This also does not enlist other family members to become involved. A good manager involves all parties in the endeavor.

Some statistical shoppers have said that every time a woman enters the store to buy four items, she picks up ten extra ones, and seven of them are unnecessary!

Just returning from a short vacation, I ran into the store to pick up four items I had jotted down. I needed them over the weekend. Since I am very conscious of planning, I did not take a basket at the door when I entered. A few minutes later, standing at the check stand and hardly able to hold onto all of my purchases, I realized what I had done. I counted and there I was—living proof with ten extra items. With today's prices, you cannot afford not to plan.

Add to your list new recipes that are similar to the favorite dishes of your family, or try them on your friends for variety. Many wives claim they do not plan because they never know when the husband will arrive or *if* he will arrive home.

Do you have children? Prepare for yourself and for them. One of the warmest places in the world is around a dinner table where time and thought have been put into the meal. It is a haven where you can share the good times of the day and let each person be important. It is also a teaching time even when husband/father is not present. Let the children know he (husband/father) misses being there. Explain how demanding his responsibility of providing for the family is for him. A man hurries to get home to this kind of an atmosphere. A mother absent occasionally is sorely missed and the family learns to move on smoothly without her because of her previous planning.

A properly-set table and a well-prepared meal set the mood for sharing. It is one of the greatest settings for building relationships. Manners are taught much more quickly and thoroughly by example than by constant verbal correction. Table talk needs to be positive. It aids digestion, builds good patterns for the family, and is enjoyable to all present. It also stores pleasant memories. When we have guests we plan and prepare our best. There is not a guest you will ever entertain as important as the family you serve every day. This kind of an attitude leaves no room for later regrets of what might have been done together.

The single career woman who becomes successful plans her schedule and gives her best. The wife who feels good about the position she has chosen plans and works her plans to her own satisfaction. She is a winner because she has defined her job and worked it to completion.

That feeling, *if I don't have some free time I will die,* need never be a wife's experience if she will realize that she is in control of her time—therefore, her freedom is in her own hands.

There is time to *be* what you decide *to be* and feel great about your accomplishments.

Strength to Build
a Good Marriage

11
Strength to Build
a Good Marriage

"The principles sound great, but how do I ever perfect just one of them?" That was Gayle's question at the close of my series of lectures on building a good marriage.

She continued, "I believe what you are saying—that liking myself is healthy, if I give love I will be able to feel the love that comes to me, that communication is necessary, and I have a very worthwhile position as wife if I will only fill it responsibly. It is the strength to build a good marriage relationship I need. How does a normal human being hold up under such strain?"

A common problem is that one month after a series of classes is completed, a woman will come to wonder why she is taking all of this responsibility to make a good marriage upon herself. Or she may come to the conclusion it is not worth the mental strain; after all her husband is doing nothing to help. It could be she will feel that it just does not work, even though she wants to change, but does not seem to be able to change.

More is called for than a desire to have a better, stronger marriage. She must want it enough to pick herself up again and again after failing, and to begin again. It takes time to get out of a deep-rutted habit. She must be patient with herself. She would give a friend another chance if that friend blew it, wouldn't she?

If another woman tells her that there is nothing to it—change is easy—she can be assured that someone else has had some success and feels encouraged. The truth is they have made it one more day and they feel good about their accomplishment. It always seems that other people make their changes so automatic with very little difficulty. What we must realize is they are struggling and failing like we are, but we are not aware of their failures—only their victories. We must learn to look at the success in our lives and keep striving, because it feels so good to be a winner.

There is one thing of which you can be sure, God did not make us without a plan. Along with the design, he gave a set of directions whereby we might find the abundant life he has provided for us. Now, with a plan and directions all I need is the strength to do what I know to do. Right? He provides that, too.

If God did not make you, then you have an extra problem. You will have to find out who did make you, so you can receive your set of instructions to live by. If you evolved, then it seems that the only choice you have is to use the trial-and-error method as you let marriage "happen" to you—and operate under your own strength.

The one and only perfect marriage was "blown" in the Garden of Eden when Eve decided to prepare dinner from the wrong tree. God offered all of the abundance, even the tree of life, to Adam and Eve, *but she chose* to seek to be equal in knowledge with God by contesting his word to her. When Eve served Adam he did not question what she was doing, but also ate. From that day to this, man has had a tendency not to trust woman and often questions what she does or says.

Disobeying God was not painful at first, but meeting him face to face later they found the relationship was marred. God did not love them any less—but he recognized they did not want to be with him. They would rather hide in the bushes than walk in the garden and share with him.

God made the first move in reaching out to Adam and Eve. He gave them instructions from *where they were* instead of *where they could have been* had they chosen to obey him.

God's love to us today is expressed in the person of Jesus Christ. He is the way to God, the truth about God, and the eternal life that each person can have, if he so desires.

Jesus Christ came into the world so I might be able to have the barrier removed from between me and God. He made it possible for me to be in a close relationship to him. God left the choice up to me. God loves me so much that he made the provision whereby the relationship could be restored.

The decision is left to me. I can accept or refuse his offer. He is not talking to us about religion or joining a church, doing good deeds, or living a good life. He is talking about beginning a personal relationship with Christ that will last forever. He is inviting us to let him forgive us of all our sin (missing the perfect), so we can go directly to God for our strength for living.

Any person who has a desire to be rightly related to God has only to invite Jesus Christ into her life. He promises that, if invited by you to come in, he will make you a child of God. The simplicity of this turns away many who like to think of themselves as intellectuals (like Eve). The plan is plain and all can understand.

So plain. Suppose a friend of yours came to visit with you and knocked at your door. You have three choices: 1) to ignore the knock, 2) to answer and have a casual talk at the door, 3) to invite the friend into your house for a visit.

Each individual has the same three choices when God reaches out to her with his offer to correct the broken relationship (forgive the sin of rebellion) between her and God. He can be ignored, met casually, or invited into your life.

When you ask Jesus Christ into your life, he comes in the presence of the Holy Spirit to be with you always under all circumstances, good or bad, here and now, and he promises to see you through this life until you come personally to be with God.

All of the Holy Spirit comes into all of you by his power, because you believe God's Word when it declares that he can put you into a new relationship as a child of God.

Why did he have his Word lived out in Jesus Christ, written out in the Bible, and his Holy Spirit put into our lives upon request? Because he loves us, wants us to be happy, and wants us to find the fullest, most meaningful life possible.

He does not instruct to hurt but to guide. He promises with each assignment he gives to provide the strength for you to carry it out. A wife has chosen her assignment. God gives the desire to be a participating follower and he also gives the strength to follow through on the assignment. Once a believer has taken God at his word, believing he wants what is best for her, she will find God's pattern to have the warmth, joy, love, and relationship she desires for her life. Being a wife to her husband by God's guidelines is the most effective place where a wife can put her love for Christ into action.

No more debt—Christ paid for my sins—all of them—relationship established with God—I belong to him—his child. Good relationships are of more value, longer-lasting, and more satisfying than things, money, education, power, position or acclaim. Your relationship with God needs to be cultivated so you can feel closer ties with him.

Don't be a hearsay believer. Strengthen your relationship by:

1) Studying God's Word daily. Begin with five minutes. Try the Gospel of John as a starter. The Bible will tell you of God's love. The Bible is God speaking to you.

A friend of mine who is a new believer was asked by a non-Christian, "How do you know that the Bible is true?" Her reply was, "All I know is what it does for me." Let His guidance do something for you.

Claim the promises that are available in the Bible. There are over 3,500 there, but they are of little value to you unless you claim them for your own. For instance, Romans 8:28 teaches that if I live my life in a close relationship to God (my part), he will work out all my experiences for good in my life (his part). He teaches in 1 John 1:9, if I admit I am in rebellion to his way and I desire to change and ask forgiveness (my part), he is faithful to restore me to a right relationship with him (his part). Every promise has a condition to be met, thus putting us in a partnership with God.

2) Communicate with God. Pray. Thank him for every good gift he has given you and is giving you day by day. Request his help in areas in which you have needs. God is concerned about everything that happens to you.

That empty feeling that God cut you off, or is not listening, or has his phone off the hook is the experience of most believers at one time or another. Does God only listen when we feel good about it, or is he always there? The writer of Hebrews says God's promise to all believers is never to leave or forsake them. Paul wrote to the Roman Christians that there is no way we can be separated from God. There is no need of begging, "Please go with me or please protect me," because he is always with you.

Many believers struggle for mountain-top experiences all of the time wanting to *feel* his presence every minute. It is not necessary to stay on a virtual high. *The fact is God is always there.* Be still. Communicate with him about where you are, what you want, how you feel, and what you need. Call for strength a day at a time as you need it, but, as in any relationship, do not forget to thank him for being with you. And praise him for all he means to you. My Catholic friends have a lovely expression they leave me, "Go with God." I might add, for that is where abundant life is.

3) Worship. Church attendance is not a synonym for worship. Worship means to praise God and stand in awe before him. There is a promise when believers come together to worship and honor Christ that he is especially present in the gathering. Worship gives strength to me because it puts my identity as God's child in perspective. This should be our experience each time we attend church. God's Word states we are not to leave this out of our lives.

4) Bible study with other believers. First John 4:1-6 gives the test that must be put to any teacher of God's Word. The person teaching must be presenting Jesus as the Son of God and Jesus as God the Son (Savior).

Believing in Christ, there is no struggle trying to be acceptable to God. I am his child and all he has for Christ, he has for me. There needs to be no fear of not being acceptable and being cut off. It is not my goodness that keeps me related to him but his grace and love for me.

Christ in me by the Holy Spirit will produce love, joy, peace, patience, gentleness, faith, meekness and self-control. He does this as you make room in your life for God's Word. The Bible is the main avenue to knowing what is right for us and what will bring us happiness and usefullness in life.

I have never known a believer who has shown continued evidence of a strong, well-disciplined life—with her priorities worked out—that was not involved in personal Bible study, group Bible study, prayer, and having fellowship with other believers.

There is Bible reading and there is Bible study. Christ promises that the Holy Spirit will teach us from God's Word. I know many Christians who are seeking a divine revelation on their own, hoping to experience a deeper life and commitment. His Word is his instruction for that deeper life, with power to live it, given to those who are seeking. Prayer is our communicating with God. This communication also requires listening. "Be still and know that I am God" is a point most believers are overlooking.

Fellowship with other believers includes sharing experiences and problems, praying together, and studying God's Word together. The early church was set up for this purpose. Because every new believer is like a new-born baby, she has needs. She is not able to provide for herself alone. She must have the warmth of love and caring from more mature believers. She must learn a little at a time.

What happens to God's chain of command with the husband as leader when he is not a Christian? The easy answer is immediately given that he is no longer the leader. He is not "spiritual," so the wife should take over in this area. *Not so!* The Bible is very candid in 1 Peter 3:1 as it teaches the believing wife to fit her schedule around her husband, and to live her life out before God, all the while loving her husband (her part). God promises to deal directly with her husband about his responsibilities. Notice that this is not done with much speaking, *but* with doing what God has said for a wife to do.

Her assignment is to be submissive to her own husband. To me that means she is to show her love for God by loving her husband. She is to work out her relationship with her husband, realizing God loves him as much as he does her. Husband and wife working together is a number one priority according to God. It takes precedent over all other activities.

What we see most often is a believing wife interpreting God's will as an entity separate and apart from her commitment to her husband. Hence, the husband spends all of his time trying to lead his wife, and has little time left to think about his relationship to God. God waits for her to be His representative that He can operate through as an example of what His love is like.

With God's encouragement, strength from within, and a determination to be in control of her own life by His pattern, every woman *can be* happy.

Becoming What You Want to Be

12
Becoming What You Want to Be

A person IS who she IS
IS what she has BECOME
Has BECOME what she WILL

You have chosen to be a wife.

You are as happy with your definition of wife as you have decided to be. You *can become* what *you want to be.*

The hang-ups we have are involved in the difference between knowing what to do and doing what we know. Last summer our family spent ten days in Northern California on a beautiful lake. My new son-in-law, who is a very good athlete in several sports, sought to teach me to water ski. I didn't have muscle tone or coordination or a love of water, but I really did desire to participate and learn.

Knowing my family cared for me, I was sure they were not trying to drown me at first. Later I was not so sure.

There I was, afraid of water in an eight-foot-pool, and they were asking me to get out of the boat into water that is two hundred feet deep! With fish and snakes and no telling what else! At that point I was offered a second life jacket to abate my fright. Reassured, I eased off into the water hanging onto the boat for my life.

Thirty minutes later, with instructions from the boat you would not believe, I still did not have my skis on . . . because I was trying to put them on without getting my head wet! With insistence that I must become totally involved (head too) I managed to get both skis on and position the rope and give the nod that I was ready to try.

A few seconds later I was struggling face down in the water and was quite sure this was the end of my life. My family failed to inform me I could not scream with my mouth wide open, when I was falling face forward, without swallowing half the lake. Seeing me struggling face down, they yelled as they swung the boat around, "Turn over."

Now, I am on my way to becoming a trick skier. I have learned: 1) how to keep from drowning (turn over—face up); 2) to trust the life jacket to hold me up (I will not go to the bottom of the lake if I jump off the boat into the water); 3) that there is an easy way to put the skis on (getting head wet); 4) that I need to develop my muscles to be able to hold onto the rope and stand up (a year's program of exercise).

Just knowing what to do and how it should be done is not enough. "Psyching" myself up with all of the positive thinking I can muster cannot get me up on those skis. Wanting to learn to ski and believing I can learn are a beginning. I must make plans to become physically strong and follow through, or I will still be trying, but not have the strength to succeed. To wish or to think does not a skier make.

When the Apostle Paul said, "That which I want to do I don't do . . ." he seems to me to be saying that just because I have made a decision to do something, does not mean that it is settled as a fact in my life.

Is this kind of psyching ourselves up necessary because of our day to day pattern of life? As we think, so we do! If this is true, we often think one thing and try to do another much of the time. So, when we want to do what we *think*, it is almost impossible.

I can see a way to break this kind of a habit. If we entertain only the thoughts that are consistent with the way we want to behave, then we can be assured of our conduct at all times. A good illustration of this is in dieting. If I keep thinking that it is not worth the time and effort, before long I will be acting as if it is not worth my time and effort. My diet will be shot.

This can be carried through beautifully in our relationships. "Pretty is as pretty does" does not go to the source. Pretty *is* as pretty *thinks*, because that is the way to *act* pretty.

Jesus made a heavy emphasis in his message from the mountain when he taught that the beginning of all wrong actions is in the way we think.

To become "a sweet little old lady" that is a delight to be around is my goal. Becoming what *you* want to be takes thought and action today. The choice is yours.

Several years ago I was working in my church as the director of education and noticed an astounding attitude. Some of the women had a "I'm-forty-and-I'm-finished attitude." They were no longer willing to teach a Sunday School class, to sponsor a youth group, to serve on a committee, or, for the most part, even to be cooperative. I observed further and found this was their attitude toward husband, children, neighbors, and the world in general.

Concerned because I had seen this in many women, I spoke with my family doctor about it when I was having my annual physical. He said to me, "You are who you are. If you are cross, hateful and ugly on the inside now, it will come out sooner or later." It is true there are physical changes going on in the body at the fortyish age, but there are changes going on at eighteen. Does age mean a woman is no longer in control? Not if she wants to be in control.

She cannot afford to wait until she has arrived at retirement to begin this control. Why? She has stored too many resentments along the way that may explode at any moment.

If she is not in charge of herself, she reminds me of a building that is being prepared for demolition. I watched on the news in amazement as an earthquake-damaged V.A. Hospital was prepared by demolition experts. They strategically placed the explosives in small amounts throughout that building. When it was all ready it was set off by one switch. The building caved in from within and was left a heap of rubble.

To me, this is a graphic picture of what happens when we fail to deal with our displeasures as they occur. When we decide they will go away by themselves, we neatly tuck away a small resentment which is not dangerous alone. As time moves on and we continue to store away these small exasperations, our lives become full of bitterness. Along comes a seemingly small irritation and the quiet-mannered, nice, gentle person is destroyed. The newspapers publish reports daily as murder, suicide, and emotional breakdown are called to our attention.

Choices are: *construction* by refusing to store any animosity by dealing with it today . . . or *destruction* of self and/or others by not dealing with it, or by trying to say that "it will go away," or even worse that there are no displeasures in one's life (only to be storing them away).

Old age will claim the relationship a woman has spent a lifetime building. A warm, caring, interested, sharing life says love. A cold, disinterested, selfish, always-claiming-one's-own-rights life has hate as its reward.

We cannot lay claim to a good relationship as we grow older if that relationship has not been in the building process. However, it is never too late to begin to build. I have a friend who at seventy-five decided to accept Christ and claim abundant life by following his plan for a happy life. She says, "If I had only known how! I knew there had to be more. I'm just thankful I have a little time to enjoy marriage from God's pattern." She is just beginning to get acquainted with her husband and enjoy being with him after over fifty years of "existing" together.

The going rate for every wife is one hundred per cent. How could fifty per cent ever be satisfying or fulfilling?

Set a goal now. Make a plan of how you are going to build your relationship with your husband. Work with one area at a time. Too much change too fast is too discouraging. It gives that *I can't do it—it doesn't work for me* feeling. Begin at the beginning by learning to like who you are. That will add enough zest to your relationship to encourage you.

You are what *you* have to *give* to the marriage.

Husband and wife are the only two that can find the answers and solutions to marriage as it relates to them. I have offered what I believe God to be teaching us in the Scriptures. I have offered applications I have found helpful in my own marriage.

It takes two to make a marriage. I have spoken *only* to your part as a *wife* because it is your side of the court.

Marriage is two people working together to achieve mutually-defined goals.

My prayer is found in Psalm 101:2 (*The Living Bible, Paraphrased*), "I will try to walk a blameless path, but how I need your help, especially in my own home, where I long to act as I should."

Recommended Reading List

ANDREWS, GINI. *Your Half of the Apple.* Grand Rapids, Michigan: Zondervan Publishing House, n.d.

BARRETT, ETHEL. *Don't Look Now.* Glendale, Calif.: Regal Books, 1968.

BIRD, LOIS. *How to Be a Happily Married Mistress.* New York: Doubleday, 1970.

BRIGGS, DOROTHY. *Your Child's Self-esteem,* New York: Doubleday, 1970.

CARNEGIE, DALE. *How to Win Friends and Influence People.* New York: Pocket Cardinal, 1940.

CHRISTENSEN, LARRY. *The Christian Family.* Minneapolis: Bethany Fellowship, Inc., 1970.

DUVALL, EVELYN MILLIS. *Evelyn Duvall's Handbook for Parents.* Nashville: Broadman Press, 1974.

DEUTSCH, RONALD M. *The Key to Feminine Response in Marriage.* New York: Random House, 1968.

DRAKEFORD, JOHN W. *Games Husbands and Wives Play.* Nashville: Broadman Press, 1970.

_____. *Made for Each Other.* Nashville: Broadman Press, 1973.

_____. *The Awesome Power of the Listening Ear.* Waco: Word Books, 1967.

EDENS, DAVID. *The Changing Me.* Nashville: Broadman Press, 1973.

HARRIS, THOMAS A. *I'm OK—You're OK.* New York: Harper and Row, 1967.

HARTY, ROBERT AND ANNELLE. *Made to Grow.* Nashville: Broadman Press, 1973.

HENDRICKS, HOWARD G. *Say It With Love.* Wheaton, Illinois:

Victor Books, 1972.

_____. *Heaven Help the Home.* Wheaton, Illinois: Victor Books, 1973.

HOLMES, MARJORIE. *I've Got to Talk to Somebody, God.* Old Tappan, New Jersey: Fleming H. Revell Company, 1971. (Spire ed.)

HOWELL, JOHN C. *Teaching Your Children About Sex.* Nashville: Broadman Press, 1973.

HUNTER, CHARLES AND FRANCES. *How to Make Your Marriage Exciting.* Glendale, Calif.: Regal Books, 1972.

LAHAYE, TIM. *How to Be Happy Though Married.* Wheaton, Illinois: Tyndale House, 1968.

LARSON, BRUCE. *Marriage Is for Living.* Grand Rapids, Michigan: Zondervan Publishing House, 1968.

LESTER, ANDREW. *Sex Is More Than a Word.* Nashville: Broadman Press, 1973.

MCMILLEN, S. I. *None of These Diseases.* Old Tappan, New Jersey: Fleming H. Revell Company, 1968.

MALTZ, MAXWELL. *The Magic Power of Self-image Psychology.* New York: Pocket Books, 1970.

MARSHALL, CATHERINE. *Beyond Ourselves.* New York: McGraw-Hill Book Company, 1961.

MILES, HERBERT J. *Sexual Happiness in Marriage.* Grand Rapids, Michigan: Zondervan Publishing House, 1967.

_____. *Sexual Understanding Before Marriage.* Grand Rapids, Michigan: Zondervan Publishing House, 1971.

MILLER, KEITH. *The Taste of New Wine.* Waco: Word Books, 1965.

MORGAN, MARABEL. *The Total Woman.* Old Tappan, New Jersey: Fleming H. Revell Company, 1973.

OSBORNE, CECIL. *The Art of Understanding Yourself.* New York: New Family Library, 1972.

PETERSEN, EVELYN R. AND J. ALLAN. *For Women Only.* Wheaton, Illinois: Tyndale House, 1974.

PETERSEN, J. ALLAN. *The Marriage Affair.* Wheaton, Illinois: Tyndale House, 1971.

POWELL, JOHN. *Why Am I Afraid to Tell You Who I Am?* Chicago:

154

Argus Communications Company, 1969.

PRICE, EUGENIA. *Woman to Woman.* Grand Rapids: Zondervan
Publishing House, n.d.

_____. *Make Love Your Aim.* Grand Rapids: Zondervan
Publishing House, 1966.

RUBIN, THEODORE ISAAC. *The Angry Book.* New York: Collier
Books, 1970.

SHEDD, CHARLIE W. *Letters to Karen.* Old Tappan, New Jersey:
Fleming H. Revell, 1965.

TAYLOR, JACK. *The Key to Triumphant Living.* Nashville: Broadman
Press, 1970.

_____. *One Home Under God.* Nashville: Broadman Press,
1974.

WOOD, FRED M. *Growing a Life Together.* Nashville: Broadman
Press, 1975.